Women, Salvation, and Childbearing

Women, Salvation, and Childbearing

The Mystery of 1 Timothy 2:11–15

KENNETH L. WATERS SR.

◆PICKWICK *Publications* • Eugene, Oregon

WOMEN, SALVATION, AND CHILDBEARING
The Mystery of 1 Timothy 2:11–15

Copyright © 2022 Kenneth L. Waters Sr. All rights reserved. Except for brief quotations in critical publications or reviews, no part of this book may be reproduced in any manner without prior written permission from the publisher. Write: Permissions, Wipf and Stock Publishers, 199 W. 8th Ave., Suite 3, Eugene, OR 97401.

Pickwick Publications
An Imprint of Wipf and Stock Publishers
199 W. 8th Ave., Suite 3
Eugene, OR 97401

www.wipfandstock.com

PAPERBACK ISBN: 978-1-6667-3738-7
HARDCOVER ISBN: 978-1-6667-9674-2
EBOOK ISBN: 978-1-6667-9675-9

Cataloguing-in-Publication data:

Names: Waters, Kenneth L., Sr.

Title: Women, Salvation, and Childbearing : The Mystery of 1 Timothy 2:11–15 / Kenneth L. Waters Sr.

Description: Eugene, OR: Pickwick Publications, 2022 | Includes bibliographical references and index.

Identifiers: ISBN 978-1-6667-3738-7 (paperback) | ISBN 978-1-6667-9674-2 (hardcover) | ISBN 978-1-6667-9675-9 (ebook)

Subjects: LCSH: Women—Biblical teaching | Bible.—Timothy, 1st.—II, 11–15—Criticism, interpretation, etc. | Sex role—Biblical teaching | Equality—Biblical teaching | Bible.—Pastoral Epistles—Criticism, interpretation, etc.

Classification: BS2745.2 W38 2022 (paperback) | BS2745.2 (ebook)

07/07/22

Dedication
to
Deborah Tarver Waters
my wife
and the love of my life

Contents

Permissions		ix
Abbreviations		xi
Introduction		xix
1	Revealing the Mystery: Virtues as Children	1
2	Exploring the Background: The World of Timothy and Paul	18
3	Viewing the Landscape: Literature and Location	34
4	Widening the View: Theology and History	42
5	Tying in the Theme: Women in the Letters of Paul	53
6	Affirming the Author: The Undying Debate	79
7	Waiting for Vindication: The Bible and African American Women	91
8	Expecting Better: Responding to Critics	105

Contents

Appendix: Exploring Further: *Teknogonía* in Classical Literature	111
Bibliography	115
Subject-Name Index	123
Ancient Document Index	133

Permissions

I am grateful to the *Journal of Biblical Literature* and Production Manager Nicole L. Tilford for permission to reprint, revise, and expand upon portions of my article, "Saved through Childbearing: Virtues as Children in 1 Timothy 2:11-15," *Journal of Biblical Literature* 123 (2004) 703-35 for print and electronic editions of this book.

I am grateful to the *Lexington Theological Quarterly* and Editor Jerry Sumney for permission to reprint, revise, and expand upon portions of my article, "Revisiting Virtues as Children: 1 Timothy 2:15 as Centerpiece for an Egalitarian Soteriology," *Lexington Theological Quarterly* 42 (2007) 37-49 for print and electronic editions of this book.

Unless otherwise noted, all translations of ancient texts are mine. I have nevertheless consulted the English translations of the Loeb editions of Plato and Philo as well as the English translations found in Cooper and Hutchinson, *Plato: Complete Works* and Yonge, *The Works of Philo*. In the citing of passages, I retain the numbering system found in the Loeb editions. All emphases are mine unless otherwise indicated.

Abbreviations

1 Clem	1 Clement
1QH	*Hodayot* (Thanksgiving Hymns from Qumran Cave 1)
1QM	War Scroll from Qumran Cave 1
1QS	Rule of the Community from Qumran Cave 1
3 Bar	3 Baruch
3 Cor	3 Corinthians (in the NTA)
4Q	The Dead Sea Scrolls from Qumran Cave 4
ABC	*Africa Bible Commentary*. Edited by Tokunboh Adeyemo. Grand Rapids: Zondervan, 2006
Abr.	Philo, *De Abrahamo* (On the Life of Abraham)
AB	Anchor Bible
ACCS	Ancient Christian Commentary on Scripture
AD or A.D.	*Anno domini* (in the year of our Lord)
Aet.	Philo, *De aeternitate mundi* (On the Eternity of the World)
Agr.	Philo, *De agricultura* (On Agriculture)
Anim.	Philo, *De animalibus* (Whether Animals Have Reason)

Abbreviations

ANRW	*Aufstieg und Niedergang der römischen Welt: Geschichte und Kultur Rom im Spiegel der neueren Forschung*
ANTC	Abingdon New Testament Commentaries
Apoc. Adam	*Apocalypse of Adam* (In the Nag Hammadi Codices)
Apoc. Ab	*Apocalypse of Abraham*
AUSDDS	Andrews University Seminary Doctoral Dissertation Series
BC or B.C.	Before Christ
BCBC	Believers Church Bible Commentary
BCE	Before the Common Era
BDAG	Bauer, Walter, F. W. Danker, William F. Arndt, and F. Wilbur Gingrich. *A Greek-English Lexicon of the New Testament and Other Early Christian Literature*. 3rd ed. University of Chicago Press, 1999
BDB	Brown, Francis, S. R. Driver, and C. A. Briggs. *Hebrew and English Lexicon of the Old Testament*. Oxford: Clarendon, 1976
Bell.civ.	Appian, *Bella civilia* (Civil Wars)
Bibl. hist.	Diodorus Siculus, *Bibliotheca historica* (Library of History)
BibNot	*Biblische Notizen*
BTB	*Biblical Theology Bulletin*
CBQ	*Catholic Biblical Quarterly*
CC	Calvin's Commentaries
CCEGP	*The Cambridge Companion to Early Greek Philosophy*
CD	The Damascus Document from Qumran Cave 1
CE	Common Era
CECPE	*A Critical and Exegetical Commentary on The Pastoral Epistles*
Cher.	Philo, *De cherubim* (On the Cheribim)
Civ.	Augustine, *De Civitate Dei* (The City of God)

Abbreviations

CMG	Galen, *Corpus Medicorum Graecorum*
Conf.	Philo, *De confusione linguarum* (On the Confusion of Tongues)
Congr.	Philo, *De congressu eruditionis gratia* (On the Preliminary Studies)
Contempl.	Philo, *De vita contemplativa* (On the Contemplative Life)
COQG	Christian Origins and the Question of God
Corp. herm.	*The Corpus Hermeticum*
Crass.	Plutarch, *Crassus*
Crat.	Plato, *Cratylus*
Descr.	Pausanias, *Graeciae description* (Description of Greece)
Det.	Philo, *Quod deterius potiori insidari solent* (That the Worse Attacks the Better)
Deus	Philo, *Quod Deus sit immutabilis* (That God Is Unchangeable)
DNTB	*Dictionary of New Testament Background*. Edited by Craig A. Evans and Stanley E. Porter. Downer Grove, IL: IVP, 2000
DPL	*Dictionary of Paul and his Letters.* Edited by Gerald F. Hawthorne, Ralph P. Martin, and Daniel G. Reid. Downer Grove, IL: IVP, 1993
Ebr.	Philo, *De ebrietate* (On Drunkenness)
Eccl. hier.	Pseudo-Dionysius, *Ecclesiastical Hierarchy*
EGHT	*Encyclopedia of Greece and the Hellenic Tradition*
EM	*Ethics and Medics*
Eth. nic.	Aristotle, *Ethica nichomaches* (Nichomachean Ethics)
Eth. eud.	Aristotle, *Ethica eudemia* (Eudemian Ethics)
ETL	*Ephemerides Theologicae Lovanienses* (Louvain Journal of Theology and Canon Law)

xiii

Abbreviations

Exeg. Soul	*Exegesis of the Soul* (from the Nag Hammadi Codices)
ExpTimes	*Expository Times*
Fug.	Philo, *De fuga et inventione* (On Flight and Finding)
Gig.	Philo, *De gigantibus* (On Giants)
Great Pow	*Concept of Our Great Power* (in the Nag Hammadi Codices)
Haer.	Irenaeus, *Adversus haereses* (Against Heresies)
HBT	*Horizons in Biblical Theology*
Her.	Philo, *Quis rerum divinarum heres sit* (Who Is the Heir?)
Hist. eccl.	Eusebius, *Historia ecclesiastica* (Ecclesiastical History)
Hist. rom	Appian, *Historia romana* (History of Rome)
Hymn. Apoll.	Callimachus, *Hymnus in Apollinem* (Hymn to Apollo)
Hymn. Dian.	Callimachus, *Hymnus in Diana* (Hymn to Diana)
ICC	International Critical Commentary
Il.	Homer, *Illiad*
Inst.	Quintilian, *The Institutio Oratoria*
Interp Know	*Interpretation of Knowledge* (in the Nag Hammadi Codices)
Ios	Philo, *De Iosophos* (On the Life of Joseph)
IVP	InterVarsity Press
IWPR	Institute of Women's Policy Research
JBL	*Journal of Biblical Literature*
JETS	*Journal of the Evangelical Theological Society*
JFSR	*Journal of Feminist Studies in Religion*
JSNT	*Journal for the Study of the New Testament*
L.A.B.	Pseudo-Philo, *Liber Antiquitatum Biblicarum* (Biblical Antiquities)
Lach	Plato, *Laches*
LCL	Loeb Classical Library

ABBREVIATIONS

LectioD	*Lectio Difficilior*
Leg. 1, 2, 3	Philo, *Legum allegoriae* I, II, III (Allegorical Interpretation 1,2, 3)
Leg.	Plato, *Leges* (Laws)
Legat.	Philo, *Legatio ad Gaium* (On the Embassy to Gaius)
Let. Aris.	*Letter of Aristeas*
LSJ	Liddell, Henry George, Robert Scott, and H. S. Jones. *A Greek-English Lexicon.* Oxford: Clarendon, 1977
LTQ	*Lexington Theological Quarterly*
LXX	The Septuagint (Greek translation of the Hebrew Scriptures, 3rd cent. BCE)
Lysis	Plato, *Lysis*
Menex	Plato, *Menexenus*
Metam.	Apuleius, *Metamorphoses* (The Golden Ass)
Metaph.	Aristotle, *Metaphysica* (Metaphysics)
Migr.	Philo, *De migratione Abrahami* (On the Migration of Abraham)
Min.	Plato, *Minos*
MT.	The Massoretic Text of the Hebrew Scriptures, 6th-10th cent. CE
Mur. ca.	*The Muratorian Canon*
Mut.	Philo, *De mutatione nominum* (On the Change of Names)
NAB	New American Bible
Neot.	*Neotestamentica*
NET	New English Translation
NHC	Nag Hammadi Codices
NHL	*The Nag Hammadi Library in English.* Edited by James M. Robinson. 3rd ed. New York: HarperCollins, 1988
NIB	*New Interpreter's Bible.* Edited by Leander E. Keck et al.

ABBREVIATIONS

NICNT	New International Commentary on the New Testament
NIV	New International Version
NovT	*Novum Testamentum*
NRSV	New Revised Standard Version
NTA	*New Testament Apocrypha.* Edited by Wilhelm Schneemelcher and R. McL. Wilson. Louisville: Westminster/John Knox Press, 1991
NTL	New Testament Library
NTS	*New Testament Studies*
NTT	New Testament Theology
NT	New Testament
Od.	Homer, *Odyssey*
ODCC	*Oxford Dictionary of the Christian Church.* Edited by F. L. Cross and E. A. Livingstone. 2nd. ed. New York: Oxford University Press, 1974
Odes Sol	Odes of Solomon
Opif.	Philo, *De opificio mundi* (On the Creation of the World)
Orig. World	*On the Origin of the World* (in the Nag Hammadi Codices)
OTP	*Old Testament Pseudepigrapha.* Edited by James H. Charlesworth. 2 vols. New York: Doubleday, 1985
Paraph. Shem.	*Paraphrase of Shem* (in the Nag Hammadi Codices)
Phaed	Plato, *Phaedrus*
Phil.	Polycarp, *Letter to the Philippians* (not to be confused with Paul's letter to the Philippians)
Pis.	Cicero, *In Pisonem* (Against Piso)
Plato Rep.	Plato, *Republic* 588A–589B (in the Nag Hammadi Codices)
Plant.	Philo, *De plantation* (On Planting)
Pol.	Aristotle, *Politicia* (Politics)

Abbreviations

Post.	Philo, *De posteritate Caini* (On the Posterity of Cain)
Prob.	Philo, *Quod omnis probus liber sit* (That Every Good Person Is Free)
Prog.	*Progymnasmata*
Prot.	Plato, *Protagoras*
PRS	*Perspectives in Religious Studies*
Ps.-Phoc.	*Pseudo-Phocylides*
Pss. Sol.	*Psalms of Solomon*
QG	Philo, *Quaestiones et solutiones in Genesin* (Questions and Answers on Genesis)
Resp.	Plato, *Respublica* (Republic)
RevExp	*Review & Expositor*
RHP	Routledge History of Philosophy
Rom. hist.	Cassius Dio, *Historia Roma* (Roman History)
RSV	Revised Standard Version
Sacri.	Philo, *De sacrificiis Abelis et Caini* (On the Sacrifices of Cain and Abel)
SBL	Society of Biblical Literature
SBLWGRW	SBL Writings from the Greco Roman World
SCJ	*Stone-Campbell Journal*
ScrB	*Scripture Bulletin*
Sobr.	Philo, *De sobrietate* (On Sobriety)
Somn.	Philo, *De somniis* (On Dreams)
Spec.	Philo, *De specialibus legibus* (On the Special Laws)
SRWT	*Stony the Road We Trod: African American Biblical Interpretation*. Edited by Cain Hope Felder. Minneapolis: Fortress, 1991
Strom	Clement of Alexandria, *Stromata* (Miscellanies)
Symp	Plato, *Symposium*

Abbreviations

T. Ab.	*Testament of Abraham*
T. Jud.	*Testament of Judah*
T. Levi	*Testament of Levi*
Teach Silv	*The Teachings of Silvanus* (in the Nag Hammadi Codices)
Theaet.	Plato, *Theaetetus*
Theog.	Hesiod, *Theogony*
Them.	*Themelios*
Thg.	Plato, *Theages*
Tim.	Plato, *Timaeus*
TNL	*True to Our Native Land: An African American New Testament Commentary.* Edited by Brian K. Blount. Minneapolis: Fortress, 2007
Trin.	Augustine, *De Trinitate* (The Trinity)
Tri. Trac.	*Tripartite Tractate* (in the Nag Hammadi Codices)
TynBul	*Tyndale Bulletin*
USFISFCJ	University of South Florida International Studies in Formative Christianity and Judaism
VC	*Vigiliae Christianae*
Vel Exp.	*A Valentinian Exposition* (in the Nag Hammadi Codices)
Virt.	Philo, *De Virtutibus* (On the Virtues)
Virt.vit.	Aristotle, *De virtutibus et vitiis* (Virtues and Vices)
WBC	Word Biblical Commentary
WGRW	Writings from the Greco-Roman World
Wis	Wisdom of Solomon

Introduction

This book is a merger and expansion of two previously published articles, "Saved through childbearing: Virtues as Children in 1 Timothy 2:11–15," and "Revisiting Virtues as Children: 1 Timothy 2:15 as Centerpiece for an Egalitarian Soteriology." A version of the first article was presented in the 2004 International Meeting of the SBL in Groningen, Netherlands, and a version of the second in the 2007 annual meeting of the SBL in San Diego, California. I wrote the second article in order to call attention to additional Jewish and Early Christian sources for my argument. Although I did draw upon such texts in my first article, there were a few that I neglected. With the two articles, I wanted to provide adequate overview of a wide range of Greco-Roman, Jewish, and Early Christian sources for the case I was making, especially since I pursue a maverick interpretation of 1 Tim 2:11–15.

The two articles nevertheless remain ensconced in scholarly journals, and are therefore not likely to catch the eye of general readers. By reproducing my insights in book form, I hope to reach a larger audience. I reproduce some parts of the articles word for word, because I find no better ways to make the point. However, in this book there is still some rearranging of material, and some new

INTRODUCTION

material altogether. Moreover, I have transliterated and translated all ancient language words and phrases.

I also expand upon and carry forward insights that I shared in my instructional video *Mobile Ed: NT 225: Survey of the Pastoral Epistles*. I am grateful to Logos Bible Software for the opportunity to explore the significance of the Pastoral Epistles with a wide-ranging audience.

I also want to thank the students who were with me at Azusa Pacific University in a class I taught over the course of many years called *The Prison and Pastoral Epistles*. I have no doubt that my experience with them accounts in large part for the shape of this book.

Few texts have caused as much anguish and pain in the Christian community and the rest of the world as 1 Tim 2:11–15. To this day the situation has not abated. Women have especially been impacted by the seemingly prohibitive and restrictive lines drawn by the passage; and if women have been negatively impacted by this text, everyone has, whether they know it or not. However, we have to step back and ask if it is the text or the way we have approached the text that is the problem. This is where this study joins the discussion. A new insight has emerged in my encounter with this text that suggests that it is not the text, but the way the text has been read that is the problem. Further discoveries suggest that there is a body of evidence that summons us to the way the text should be read, and it is radically different from the way the text has been read. This, of course, is a matter that must be proven. I attempt to do this in the pages that follow.

My argument is original. If I must say so myself, nothing like it has appeared in the history of biblical interpretation. As I point out, Augustine leaned in the direction of my argument, but he provided no historical or literary grounding. Moreover, he missed the point of the biblical author's use of the term "childbearing." Because of its original, maverick character, my argument requires a rather detailed defense.

In the first chapter, I show why 1 Tim 2:11–15 is an intentional allegory that purposely uses "childbearing" as a metaphor for the manifestation of virtue. I then show, in the second chapter, that the

Introduction

theme of the soul giving birth to virtue or vice was a commonplace in the literary world of Timothy and Paul.

In the third chapter, we see the theme of virtues and vices as children occurring elsewhere in early Christian literature, and in Ephesian culture. The allegorical message of 1 Tim 2:11–15 coheres with the larger theological vision of the Pastoral Epistles, as I show in chapter four. In the history of Christian thought, Augustine came closer than anyone to grasping that message.

In the fifth chapter, I show that my interpretation of 1 Tim 2:11–15 coheres with Paul's egalitarian practices throughout the letters of Paul. The "virtues as children" theme is consistent with how women are viewed in the Pauline literature regardless of the debate over authorship.

In the sixth chapter, I address the issue of the authorship of the Pastoral Epistles. It is not critical for the shape of my argument in the previous chapters, but it is still a relevant issue for anyone working with these letters. It is an opportunity to contribute to an ongoing debate, therefore I took the opportunity.

In the seventh chapter, I show the relevance of this study to the contemporary issue of justice and healing for women, particularly African American women. This is a response to a call that is becoming increasingly more urgent—a call to move beyond mere exegesis to engagement with ongoing social challenges.

In the eighth chapter, I reluctantly address some shortfall in the way previous versions of this study have been received in the biblical studies guild. After I first presented the central argument of this book at the International SBL in Groningen, one of the other presenters in the session said to me privately, "This will change everything." I was encouraged by her remark. However, many scholars over the years have appeared off put by the publication of my research. I think it is because of the destabilizing impact my study has in the field of Pauline Studies, especially in the study of the Pastoral Epistles. I do not think this justifies the attempt to ignore my research, which, of course, would be a way of suppressing it. I therefore have no choice but to call out these attempts. I finally attach an appendix to show that the Greek term for "childbearing" is not

INTRODUCTION

idiosyncratic, eccentric, nor particularly metaphorical, although used metaphorically in 1 Timothy.

I am grateful to editors Matthew Wimer, EJ Davila, and Robin Parry of Wipf and Stock Publishers for their confidence in this project. Their support and encouragement are rich affirmation and vindication of countless hours spent excavating primary sources and formulating a coherent case for a new hermeneutic. I also extend heartfelt thanks to typesetter Savanah N. Landerholm for her assiduous work while giving shape to this book.

I also wish to express my gratitude for the late Gail O'Day who was editor of the *JBL* when my foundational article for this book was published. In fact, two of my articles were published in *JBL* under her watch. She saw the potential in my studies even though they went against the scholarly consensus, and she felt that they should have a platform in *JBL*. I will always cherish the memory of her sponsorship.

My colleagues and co-workers at Azusa Pacific University and Azusa Pacific Seminary continue to be an encouragement to me. Many of them were the first to hear the argument that forms the core of this book. I am grateful for the home that they have provided for my academic sharing, growth, and nurture.

Through the publication of this book, I celebrate the memory of my late academic mentors William R. Farmer and Virgil Howard of Perkins School of Theology, Southern Methodist University, and David Scholer of Fuller Theological Seminary, all world–class scholars of the New Testament. I see this publication as a salute to their investment in me.

I thank my wife Deborah for her companionship and support through the years. The effort spent achieving progress in one's professional life and calling leads to some measure of fulfillment, but it still may not be enough for at least some of us. In my case, more is definitely needed and my wife Deborah has provided that. I therefore celebrate her presence in my life. The dedication of this book to her is a small installment on the debt of gratitude I owe to her.

1

Revealing the Mystery
Virtues as Children

> Let a woman learn in silence in all subjection. I do not permit a woman to teach nor to exercise authority over a man, but to be in silence. For Adam was formed first, then Eve. And Adam was not deceived, but the woman being deceived fell into transgression. Yet *she* will be saved through *childbearing*, if *they* continue in faith, and love, and holiness with temperance.
>
> (1 TIM 2:11–15)

A PIVOTAL DISCOVERY

Philo of Alexandria (20 BCE–50 CE) is not in the Bible, but he writes about the Bible. He belongs to a large category called extrabiblical literature. Yet reading Philo is important for those of us who also read and interpret the Bible, particularly for those of us who read and interpret the Letters of Paul. After all, Philo was an older contemporary of Paul, and like Paul, a Hellenistic Jew and interpreter of the Hebrew Scriptures. Philo gives us insight into the literary world of Paul. There are many places in their writings where Paul and Philo seem to espouse related ideas.[1]

While reading Philo over the course of some days, I began to notice a recurring theme. It had to do with the manifestation of virtue in human life and behavior. I was struck by Philo's repeated tendency to speak of this manifestation as a birth, as if the virtues so demonstrated were *children* of the soul. In a buoyant moment, my mind drifted over to a place in the Pauline corpus where the themes of childbirth and virtues also merged, 1 Tim 2:15. I became more and more intrigued with the possibility that a literary connection was present. As my investigations continued, I became aware that this "virtues as children" theme was widespread in the ancient world beyond Philo, even though it was certainly characteristic of Philo. It was also present in the Bible in places beyond 1 Tim 2:15. I also found that the obverse "vices as children" theme was equally prevalent in the same literature. I became convinced that in the literary world of Paul, 1 Tim 2:15 could be justifiably read in a way it has never been read before in the modern world. I was excited by the possibility, given both the difficulty that this verse has caused for interpreters of the New Testament, and the damage caused to both the interior and exterior lives of women by historic ways this verse has been handled in androcentric culture.

I found myself confronted with both the liberating potential, and the evidence for a new argument about the meaning of 1 Tim 2:15. Both the potential and the evidence compels me to include

---

1. For example, the war between Mind and Pleasure in Philo (*Leg.* 2.22–41) is similar to the war between spirit and flesh in Paul (Rom 8:1–17; Gal 5:16–25). Philo's treatise on circumcision (*Spec.* 1.1–11) provides some background for Paul's response to the issue (Rom 2:25–29; 4:9–12; Gal 5:1–12). Philo's reflection on slavery and Mosaic law (*Prob.* 10–18, 36–41) informs our understanding of Paul's message to slaves and slaveholders (1 Cor 7:17–24; 1 Tim 6:1–2). Both Philo and Paul evoke Deut 25:4, "you shall not muzzle the ox that treads out the corn," but for different reasons (*Virt.* 145; 1 Cor 9:9; 1 Tim 5:18). Paul's distinction between "lawful by nature Gentiles," Gentile believers in Jesus Christ, and wanton pagan Gentiles (Rom 1:18–32; 2:12–16; 11:13, 25) seems to parallel Philo's distinction between philosophical Gentiles, *proselyte* Gentiles, and wanton, pagan Gentiles (*Spec.* 1.36–37, 51–54). Both Philo (*Somn.* 2.207; *Spec.* 1.327; *Abr.* 131) and Paul (1 Cor 10:1–5; Gal 4:24; 1 Tim 2:11–15) assign legitimacy to allegorical interpretation of the Hebrew Scriptures.

the verses preceding 2:15 for context. My starting point is therefore expanded to include verses 11–15, which recalls Gen 3:1–7, 16, a passage which Philo (*Leg.* 3.198–221) also interprets in a characteristically allegorical fashion. My discovery has become the basis for a new hermeneutic.

I therefore argue that 1 Tim 2:11–15 is an allegory in which the virtues faith, love, holiness, and temperance are portrayed as the *children* of those women in Ephesus who will be saved. The case I make for this is based on literary and historical evidence. A major part of our argument will expose a metaphorical use of the term "childbearing" and related concepts in the environment of 1 Timothy. However, preliminary discussion will center on our use of the term "allegory" as a description of 1 Tim 2:11–15. We will also show why the passage is ostensibly focused on a context-specific rather than a general relationship between women and men. Our goal is nothing less than to justify an entirely new reading of the phrase "saved through childbearing" in 1 Tim 2:15.

ALLEGORY AS CATEGORY

The term "allegory" is here used in the sense of an extended metaphor, that is, in the sense of language, imagery, and structure drawn from an ancient narrative and applied to a contemporary circumstance.[2] Alan Padgett uses the term "cautionary or negative typology" in a similar sense, while Andrew C. Perriman prefers the term "figurative interpretation."[3] Both scholars refuse the simple, unqualified term "typology" in order to avoid the suggestion of "creation-order" or "prefigurative relationship" as a component of 1 Tim 2:11–15.[4] According to Perriman, prefigurement involves "statements about a state of affairs established at creation that has

---

2. See Dawson, *Allegorical Readers*, 3, 5. To distinguish allegory from "metaphor, etymology, and personification," Dawson says, "interpretations and compositions designated as 'allegorical' must have a narrative dimension."

3. Padgett, "Wealthy Women at Ephesus," 26; Perriman, "What Eve Did," 140.

4. Padgett specifically rejects the idea of "a creation-order of man over woman, and in general the superiority of man to woman" ("Wealthy Women at Ephesus," 27, 31).

prevailed to the time of this writing," while a "figurative interpretation" in this case refers only to "statements about a situation in language borrowed from Genesis."[5] Both scholars rightly discern that Gen 3:1–21 is not the archetype for divinely predetermined or prefigured relationships in the Ephesian congregation of Timothy, but only a source of meaningful language, imagery, and narration for the Ephesian situation.[6]

It would seem, however, that Padgett and Perriman's purpose would best be served by the term "allegory." If one might risk a pithy distinction, in a typology the present derives its meaning from the past, but in an allegory the past derives its meaning from the present.[7] Both Padgett and Perriman seem to find that the metaphorical meanings of 1 Tim 2:11–15 are determined by the present situation of the author and his audience.[8] There would at first seem to be no compelling reason for preferring the term "allegory" over "figurative interpretation," especially since the terms are practically synonymous. Yet the term "allegory" and its cognates have a longer history and furthermore connote a particular method of biblical interpretation contemporaneous with the Pastoral Epistles.[9] At

---

5. Perriman, "What Eve Did," 140.

6. However, for arguments from creation-order see Bassler, *1 Timothy, 2 Timothy, Titus*, 60; Gordon, "A Certain Kind of Letter," 53–63.

7. See Dawson, *Allegorical Readers*, 15–16: "Because it is said to preserve the historical reality of both the initial 'type' and its corresponding 'antitypes,' typology is said to differ from allegory, which dissolves the historical reality of type and/or antitype into timeless generalities or conceptual abstractions." Dawson, however, goes on to expound his view in which "typology is understood to be simply one species of allegory." See also Davidson, *Typology in Scripture*, 101n1: "By those who make a distinction between allegory and typology (and this is the majority of modern scholars), allegory involves an arbitrary assigning of externally imposed meaning to the words of Scripture, which meaning is foreign to the ideas conveyed by the words, and often disregards the historical sense of the passage."

8. For an unqualified typological interpretation of 1 Tim 2:11–15, see Collins, *I &II Timothy and Titus*, 76–77: "Insofar as Eve was more fully deceived than was Adam, she was the prototypical female, Adam the prototypical male."

9. The allegorical method of biblical interpretation is usually associated with Alexandria and most notably represented by Philo (20 BCE–50 CE), and in later times by Clement (150–215 CE) and Origen (185–254 CE), all of

the very least, this shows that there is nothing idiosyncratic about the author's hermeneutic in 1 Tim 2:11-15, nor about our modern attempts to characterize this hermeneutic. While the qualified typological/figurative approaches used by Padgett and Perriman illuminate our understanding of 1 Tim 2:11-15, the extended metaphorical usages in this passage seem more profitably described as allegory.

CHILDBEARING AS ALLEGORICAL METAPHOR

In this discussion, our focus is on the allegorical use of the term "childbearing" (τεκνογονία, teknogonia) in 1 Tim 2:15.[10] It is a *hapax legomenon*, that is to say, a term that only occurs once in the Greek New Testament. It is a clear application of God's pronouncement upon Eve in Gen 3:16: "I will greatly increase your sorrow and your conception and in pain you will *bear children*" (MT: תלדי בני, *tldy bny*; LXX: τέξῃ τέκνα, *texē tekna*). In 1 Tim 2:15, however, the children to be borne are to be found in the immediate context of the term, namely, the virtues faith, love, holiness, and temperance (πίστις, ἀγάπη, ἁγιασμός, and σωφροσύνη; *pistis, agapē, hagiasmos,* and *sōphrosynē*).[11] First, the women give

---

Alexandria. Cf. Cross and Livingstone, "Allegory," 42–43.

10. A form of τεκνοτροφέω, *teknotropheō* ("to bring up children"), appears in 1 Tim 5:10, while a form of τεκνογονέω, *teknogoneō* ("to bear children"), appears in 1 Tim 5:14. For more on the term τεκνογονία, *teknogonia,* see the Appendix.

11. Cf. the four cardinal virtues of Plato, *Resp.* 4.419A–445E, σωφροσύνη, ἀνδρεία, σοφία, and δικαιοσύνη (*sophrosynē, andreia, sophia,* and *dikaiosynē*). The first is variously translated by the terms temperance, moderation, self-control, sound-mindedness, and sobriety. The remaining three are usually translated respectively by courage, wisdom, and justice. In *Resp.* 3.389D, σωφροσύνη, *sophrosynē,* is central to civic order and administration. "And as for the multitudes are not the chief aims of temperance [σωφροσύνη, *sophrosynē*] to be obedient to rulers, and for rulers themselves to practice self-control in regard to drink and the pleasures of both sex [ἀφροδίσια, *aphrodisia*] and food?" The four cardinal virtues reappear in Philo, *Leg.* 1.63–72, where they are represented by the four rivers of the paradise of Eden (Gen 2:10–14), in his *Ebr.* 23, as those qualities which are cut off from those who are opposed to learning, and in *Post.* 128. For Philo, σωφροσύνη, *sophrosynē,* is necessary for the health of the soul and mental salvation. See *Virt.* 14–16:

birth to these virtues, and then they *continue* or *abide* in them in order to be saved. We see this same allegorical pattern in Philo, *Leg.* 3.3.[12] Here he interprets the birth of the Hebrew male infants at the hands of the Hebrew midwives (Exod 1:21) as the effort of the soul (ψυχή, *psychē*) to "build up the substance of virtue" (οἰκοδομοῦσι τὰ ἀρετῆς πράγματα, *oikodomousi ta aretēs pragmata*).[13] Philo then says that the substance of virtue is that "in which they have also decided to abide" (οἷς καὶ ἐνοικεῖν προῄρηνται, *ois kai enoikein proērēntai*). In each case, that which has given birth (i.e., the soul or the Ephesian women) abides in the very thing that was borne. Our warrant for seeing this sequence of birthing and abiding in 1 Tim 2:15 comes partly from 1 Tim 1:5–6. Here the virtues of love, good conscience, and faith proceed from a pure heart (καθαρὰ καρδία, *kathara kardia*), in the same way that the Philonic virtues proceed from the soul.[14] When the author criticizes those who have "missed the mark by turning aside" (ἀστοχήσαντες ἐξετράπησαν, *astochēsantes exetrapēsan*) from these virtues, he clearly implies that one should continue or abide in these virtues after they are born (cf. 1 Tim 1:19; 2 Tim 2:22). This at least shows that the author of 1 Timothy and Philo share a similar pattern of thinking in regard to virtue ethics. Elsewhere in the Pauline corpus, the idea of giving birth to and abiding in the virtues is expressed in terms of "fruit bearing" (καρποφόρος, *karpophoros*) (Rom 6:21–22; 7:4–5; Gal

---

"And the health of the soul [ὑγεία δὲ ψυχῆς, *hygeia de psychēs*] consists in well-tempered faculties... with reason in control... the special name of this healthy state is temperance [σωφροσύνη, *sophrosynē*], which perfects salvation [σωτηρίαν] in our rational being." Finally, cf. Augustine, *Civ.* 19.4.4, for his discussion of temperance, prudence, justice, and fortitude.

12. Philo describes his method of interpretation variously as ἀλληγορικός, *allēgorikos* ("allegorical" or "figurative") (*Opif.* 157), συμβολικῶς, *symbolikōs* ("symbolic") (*Opif.* 164), and τροπικῶς, *tropikōs* ("tropical" or "metaphorical") (*QG* 1.52).

13. Cf. "to build up the cause of virtue" (Colson and Whitaker, *Philo*, 303) and "to build up the actions of virtue" (Yonge, *The Works of Philo*, 50).

14. This same pattern of birthing (producing) and abiding occurs in Odes Sol 11:1–3 (c. 100–125 CE): "My heart was pruned... and it produced fruits for the Lord... and I ran in the Way in his peace, in the way of truth" (Charlesworth, "Odes of Solomon," 2:744). Notice the agricultural reproductive metaphor.

5:22-25; Eph 5:8-11; Phil 1:11; Col 1:6, 10; Titus 3:14). This is a use of agricultural rather than gynecological reproductive imagery, but the idea is fundamentally the same.[15] There is yet no grammatical element in 1 Tim 2:11-15, such as an appositive phrase or linking verb, that explicitly shows the equivalence between the four virtues mentioned and the result of childbearing. There would probably be an objection to our thesis on this basis; however, the absence of such an element in 1 Tim 2:11-15 becomes rather inconsequential in light of a similarly structured passage in the writings of Philo. In *Gig.* 5, a series of virtues is referred to as the "male children" of Noah in contrast to the vices of the disobedient multitudes, which are referred to in typical patriarchal fashion as "female children."

> For since the just Noah had male children [ἀρρενογονεῖ, *arrenogonei*], as a follower of right reason, which is perfect and truly male, the thoroughgoing injustices [ἀδικία πάντως, *adikia pantōs*] of the multitudes show them to be bearers of female children [θηλυτόκος, *thēlytokos*].

Here the children of Noah are not literal children, but those virtues that correspond to the nature of reason itself, namely, manliness,

---

15. The idea of children as "fruit of the womb" (MT: פרי־בטן, *pry-btn*; cf. LXX: ἔκγονα τῆς κοιλίας, *ekgona tēs koilias*; καρπὸν κοιλίας, *karpon koilias*) is not unfamiliar in Judaism (Gen 30:2; Deut 5:3; 7:13; 28:4, 11, 18; 30:9; Isa 13:18; Jub 20:9; 28:16; *L.A.B.* 50.2; 55.4; T.Ab. 6.5; 8.6; 2 En 71:11; cf. Hos 9:16; Luke 1:42; 2 Bar 62:5; 73:7). See also *Plant.* 134-38, where Philo uses the terms "fruit of the soul" (ὁ τῆς ψυχῆς καρπός, *ho tēs psychēs karpos*) and "offspring of the soul" (τὸ τῆς ψυχῆς γέννημα, *to tēs psychēs gennēma*) interchangeably in reference to Issachar. In this allegory, Leah represents "a rational and virtuous nature" while her sons, Judah and Issachar respectively represent "the mind which blesses God" and "the reward of gratitude." Judah is also called "the holy and praiseworthy fruit" (ἅγιος καὶ αἰνετὸς καρπός, *hagios kai ainetos karpos*). In *Sobr.* 65, Isaac is the "fruit" of Abraham. Philo frequently uses "children" (γεννήματα, παιδεία, and ἔγγονα; *gennēmata, paideia*, and *engona*) and "fruit" (καρπός, *karpos*) interchangeably as a metaphor for virtues, just as he uses "childbearing" (τίκτειν, τικτόμενος; *tiktein, tiktomenos*) and "fruit bearing" (καρποφόρος, καρποτόκα; *karpophoros, karpotoka*) interchangeably for the process of producing virtues (*Mut.* 73, 161, 224; *Somn.* 1.37; 2.75-77, 272; *Spec.* 2.29; *Prob.* 70, 160; *Contempl.* 68; *QG* 1.49; 3.10, 54; *Agr.* 9-11, 23, 25; *Opif.* 154-55; *Leg.* 1.45, 49; *Post* 10; *Sacri.* 103-04; *Gig.* 4; *Deus* 4, 166, 180; *Sobr.* 65; *Migr.* 125, 139-40, 205-6; *Congr.* 6; *Plant.* 77, 106, 126, 132, 136).

justice, perfection, and uprightness.¹⁶ Yet there is no grammatical element that explicitly identifies the children of Noah as these particular virtues. Instead, it is both the immediate and larger literary context of *Gig.* 5 that requires this identification. It is particularly in Philo, *Deus* 117–18, that the children of Noah are most clearly identified as the four virtues mentioned: "For [Moses] says, 'These are the generations of Noah [αἱ γενέσεις Νῶε, *hai geneseis Nōe*]. Noah was a just man, perfect among his generation. Noah was well-pleasing to God.'" Philo then explains that the children (ἔγγονα, *engona*) of Noah are "the virtues already mentioned" (αἱ προειρημέναι ἀρεταί, *hai proeirēmenai aretai*) here in Gen 6:9, namely, "the being a man, the being just, the being perfect, the being well-pleasing to God" (τὸ ἄνθρωπον εἶναι, τὸ δίκαιον εἶναι, τὸ τέλειον εἶναι, τὸ Θεῷ εὐαρεστῆσαι, *to anthrōpon einai, to dikaion einai, to teleion einai, to Theō euarestēsai*).¹⁷ Philo makes explicit in this passage what was implicit in *Gig.* 5. In a similar manner, it is the immediate and larger literary context of 1 Tim 2:11–15 that creates the equivalence between *children* and *virtues* in this passage (e.g., 1 Tim 1:5–6, 19; 2:10; 4:12; 2 Tim 2:22; Titus 2:11–12). In the case of 1 Tim 2:11–15, however, it is also the larger religio-philosophical context of the entire epistle that drives us toward this identification, as we shall see.

---

16. See Philo, *Mut.* 189, Arphaxad, the child of Noah (Gen 11:10) is "the offspring of the soul" (ἔγγονον ψυχῆς, *engonon psychēs*). He represents that virtue which destroys iniquity.

17. In *Gig.* 5, Noah "had male children" (ἀρρενογονεῖ, *arrenogonei*) who are associated with reason, which is "truly male" (ἄρρενα ὄντως, *arrena ontōs*). In the cognate passage, *Deus* 117–18, Noah is "a just man" (ἄνθρωπος δίκαιος, *anthrōpos dikaios*) and "the being a man" (τὸ ἄνθρωπον εἶναι, *to anthrōpon einai*) is one of his virtues. The terms ἄνθρωπος, *anthrōpos*, and τὸ ἄνθρωπον εἶναι, *to anthrōpon einai*, could very well be rendered "human" and "the being human" or "that he was human." However, context seems to limit the sense of ἄνθρωπος, *anthrōpos*, and ἄνθρωπον, *anthrōpon*, to "man," especially since the terms are so closely associated with ἄρρην, *arrēn* and refer specifically to the male Noah and the virtues that are his offspring.

Revealing the Mystery

FIRST TIMOTHY 2:11-15 AS ALLEGORY

Recognition of the allegorical character of 1 Tim 2:11–15 is forced by the author's appropriation of Gen 3:1–21, particularly his use of the names Adam and Eve, and the apparent equivalence that the author creates between the singular pronoun "she" and the plural "they" in v. 15.

> Yet *she* will be saved [σωθήσεται, *sōthēsetai*] through childbearing, if *they* continue [μείνωσιν, *meinōsin*] in faith, and love, and holiness with temperance.

"They" refers either to "she," "her children," or "Adam and Eve" in this verse. If "they" refers to "she" then the two pronouns can only be understood as metaphorical references to the women of the Ephesian congregation. Since "Eve" in this literary context is the antecedent of "she," this name can also be understood only as a metaphorical reference to the women of the Ephesian congregation. Similarly, the remark about "the woman" (ἡ γυνή, *hē gynē*) who was deceived and fell into transgression becomes a metaphorical reference to the same collective. "Adam" then, by contrast can only be a metaphorical reference to the men of the Ephesian congregation, particularly those functioning as leaders and teachers in the church.

We could then rule out the proposition that the author of 1 Timothy is speaking typologically of "women and men in general." An attentive reading of the epistle shows that the author is ostensibly concerned only with the specific situation of women and men in the church of Ephesus (e.g., 1 Tim 1:3–7, 20; 2:8–10; 3:14–15; 4:16). His use of the Genesis narrative is subordinate to this specific focus and not an attempt to delineate an universal law of creation based upon a prototypical relationship.[18] In all other places where the author draws upon the Hebrew Scriptures, it is an ostensibly context-specific application (1 Tim 5:18; 2 Tim 2:19; 3:8, 16).[19]

---

18. See Padgett, "Wealthy Women at Ephesus," 25: "It is these particular women rather than women in general that Paul was not allowing authority over men, nor teaching positions, in the church services (v. 12)."

19. The vast majority of NT scholars agree that 1 Timothy, 2 Timothy, and

If "they" refer to "her children" then we have the strange idea of Eve's salvation being dependent upon the piety of her progeny. This idea has no support anywhere in biblical tradition.[20] In fact, it is inconsistent with Deut 24:16, Jer 31:29–30, and Ezek 18:1–4. Even stranger, we would have Adam exempt from a requirement for salvation imposed only upon Eve.

If "they" refer to "Adam and Eve" then in effect, Eve's salvation becomes dependent on childbearing, and upon *both* her piety and Adam's piety. Meanwhile, Adam's salvation is dependent only upon his own piety. These also are ideas that have no precedent in biblical tradition.[21]

The metaphorical or, as I would more specifically argue, *allegorical* interpretation offers the least difficulties in the context of biblical tradition. Furthermore, understanding "she," "they," "the woman," and "Eve" as equivalent references to the women of the Ephesian church coheres with an understanding of 1 Tim 2:8—3:11 as instruction for local women.[22] Moreover, this is not the only place in the Pauline corpus where allegorical interpretations occur (Rom 11:17–24; 1 Cor 10:1–11; 13:4–7; Gal 4:22–27; Eph 6:12–17).[23]

Titus are the work of a single author. On the single authorship of the Pastoral Epistles, see Marshall and Towner, *The Pastoral Epistles*, 1–2.

20. See Dunn, "The First and Second Letters to Timothy," 802, esp. n56. See also Bassler, *1 Timothy, 2 Timothy, Titus*, 61.

21. See Mounce, *The Pastoral Epistles*, 147.

22. See Scholer, "1 Timothy 2:9–15," 196. "Eve (v. 13) represents woman (v. 14)/women (vv. 9, 10, 11); thus, the grammatically natural shift in verse 15 from the singular (woman as womankind) to the plural (individual women)." Cf. also Fee, *Gospel and Spirit*, 59. "That is exactly the point of 5:15—such deception of women by 'Satan' has already been repeated in the church in Ephesus." Both Scholer and Fee imply a metaphorical understanding of Eve in 1 Timothy 2:11–15 although they do not use terms like metaphorical, figurative, or allegorical. Both, however, stop short of a metaphorical reading of "childbearing" in 2:15.

23. Even though Paul uses the terms τύποι, *typoi* (1 Cor 10:6), and τυπικῶς, *typikōs* (1 Cor 10:11), to describe the relation of a section of the wilderness narrative (Exod 14:10—32:35) to the Corinthian believers, his application is still an ἀλληγορία, *allēgoria* (cf. ἀλληγορούμενα, *allēgoroumena* in Gal 4:24), since he is interpreting the past in light of his present, just as he does with the story of Sarah and Hagar in Gal 4:22–27. For an allegorical characterization of

The author of 1 Tim 2:11–15 therefore uses the names "Adam" and "Eve" as metaphors respectively for the male teachers and leaders of the Ephesian congregation on the one hand, and its apparently wealthy female members on the other (1 Tim 2:9).[24] As "Adam" was *formed first* (πρῶτος ἐπλάσθη, *prōtos eplasthē*) in Gen 2:7–25, so the male teachers and leaders of the Ephesian church were formed first in Christ *before* the women. The seniority of the male teachers and leaders in Christ becomes the author's reason for affirming *their* authority over those women of Ephesus who were far less mature in terms of their Christian development (not the authority of every man over every woman).[25] It was because of their immaturity in Christ that these women were being deceived by false teachers just as Eve was deceived by the serpent. They were therefore called upon to submit in silence to the instruction of more seasoned, genuine leaders. These basic points have already been persuasively argued by Padgett with affirmation by Perriman.[26]

---

1 Cor 10:4 and context, see Dawson, *Allegorical Readers*, 8. For an opposing typological interpretation of 1 Cor 10:1–13, see Davidson, *Typology in Scripture*, 287, 290. For Davidson, τύπος, *typos*, and τυπικῶς, *typikōs*, in 1 Cor 10 seemingly come close to having "specialized, technical meaning as hermeneutical terms." This, however, would probably be reading too much into Paul's use of these terms.

24. Nor is this the only place in the Pastoral Epistles where metaphorical language is used. See 2 Tim 2:3–6, 20–21; 4:6–8, although in these other places they are not allegorical usages, strictly speaking.

25. *Contra* Collins, *I & II Timothy and Titus*, 77; Bassler, *1 Timothy, 2 Timothy, Titus*, 60–61. Collins feels that the author of 1 Timothy is referring to "women in general," particularly with his statement "she will be saved." Bassler also feels that the author of 1 Timothy is addressing the behavior and weaknesses of women in general.

26. I am grateful to Professor Alan Padgett for personally providing bibliographic information concerning his own work as well as the work of Fee, Perriman, and Porter, all cited in this present chapter.

Women, Salvation, and Childbearing

A Postnatal Relationship in Literary Context

Padgett and Perriman's metaphorical interpretations appear more feasible and defensible than Richard Clark Kroeger and Catherine Clark Kroeger's treatment of 1 Tim 2:11-15 which is based upon rather loose reinterpretations of αὐθεντεῖν and ἡσυχίᾳ, *authentein* and *hēsychia* (1 Tim 2:12). Rather than understand αὐθεντεῖν, *authentein* as "to usurp authority over," the Clark Kroegers argue for translating the term as "to proclaim oneself as author of," and rather than understand ἡσυχίᾳ, *hēsychia*, as "to be in silence" they translate the word as "to be in conformity" or "to keep something a secret," so that verse 2:12 may be rendered:

> I do not permit a woman to teach nor to represent herself as originator of man but she is to be inconformity [with the scriptures] [or that she keeps it a secret]. For Adam was created first, then Eve.[27]

The author is therefore countervailing the Gnostic teaching that Eve was the creator of Adam.[28] While interesting, the Clark Kroegers' reinterpretations of αὐθεντεῖν, *authentein*, and ἡσυχίᾳ, *hēsychia*, appear rather forced.[29]

The Clark Kroegers, however, are helpful in exposing a possible Gnostic or at least proto-Gnostic presence in the background of 1 Timothy.[30] The term "proto-Gnostic" may be more appropriate since we first know of a full-blown Gnosticism only from second to fourth century texts.[31] Passages such as 1 Tim 1:3-6, 20; 5:11-15; 6:20; 2 Tim 2:14-18; 3:6-9; 4:14 (cf. Titus 3:9) are frequently cited as possible indicators of an incipient Gnosticism in the Ephesian environment.[32] This recognition of a possible proto-Gnostic pres-

---

27. Kroeger and Kroeger, *I Suffer Not A Woman*, 103, 192.
28. Kroeger and Kroeger, *I Suffer Not A Woman*, 103, 121.
29. For an incisive critique of the Clark Kroegers' argument see Perriman, "What Eve Did," 132-38. See also Marshall and Towner, *The Pastoral Epistles*, 457-66; Liefield, "Response to 1 Timothy 2:12," 244-48.
30. Kroeger and Kroeger, *I Suffer Not A Woman*, 60, 66.
31. *NHL*, 2, 16.
32. Kroeger and Kroeger, *I Suffer Not A Woman*, 59-63; *NHL*, 4.

ence suggests a direction of interpretation different from that taken by Padgett, Perriman and others, and even the Clark Kroegers themselves in regard to being "saved through childbearing."[33]

Padgett, who renders the phrase "saved through childbirth" sees the passage as a reference to Gen 3:15. The "child" is primarily the seed of Eve, and in the context of 1 Timothy perhaps an "oblique reference" to the child of Mary of Nazareth. Padgett indicates, however, that any allusion to Mary and her child is uncertain, and at best, a tangential one. In the end, the women of the Ephesian congregation are encouraged to reject the heretical doctrines of the snake-like false teachers, return to the marriage bed and resume childbearing.[34]

Perriman, too, sees in 1 Tim 2:15 an allusion to Gen 3:15. However, childbearing is only a "synecdoche" for a series of "good works," such as, "childrearing, hospitality to strangers, washing the feet of the saints, helping the afflicted," alluded to in 2:10 and 5:9–10.[35] Still, in Perriman's discussion, the literal birthing of children remains the root meaning of childbearing in 1 Tim 2:15.

Porter argues that the author "equates a woman's earthly function of bearing children with her eschatological or salvific reward."[36] By so doing the author of the epistle is countering an ascetic tendency and women's neglect of their domestic roles (1 Tim 4:3). He endorses the resumption of normal relations including those that result in childbirth.[37] Despite our discomfort, "the author of 1 Timothy apparently believed that for the woman who abides in

---

33. See Padgett, "Wealthy Women," 21; Perriman, "What Eve Did," 133. Padgett, nevertheless suggests that ascetic tendencies referred to in 1 Timothy may be behind the Gnosticism of the *Acts of Paul and Thecla* and other apocryphal acts, and therefore may be "a precursor to Gnosticism arising from heterodox Judaism." In response to the Clark Kroegers' description of false teaching in Ephesus, Perriman observes that "it is quite possible that there were Gnostic elements in it and that women played a prominent role in its dissemination."

34. Padgett, "Wealthy Women," 27–29.

35. Perriman, "What Eve Did," 140–41.

36. Porter, "What Does It Mean," 101.

37. Porter, "What Does It Mean," 102. See also Bassler who makes a similar point (*1 Timothy, 2 Timothy, Titus*, 61).

faith, love, and holiness, her salvation will come by the bearing of children."[38]

The Clark Kroegers particularly see in 1 Tim 2:15 a repudiation of Gnostic doctrines forbidding childbearing. They observe: "Women are acceptable to God within their childbearing function and need not change their sexual identity to find salvation." They find it best to render the statement as, "she shall be saved within the childbearing function" to emphasize that "woman can be saved while she still possesses that distinctive which most decisively sets her apart from man."[39]

For Simon Coupland, only one interpretation makes sense in the context of 1 Timothy and Pauline and "Deutero-Pauline" teaching on salvation through faith in Christ, and that is to take the prepositional object of *dia* (διά) in 1 Tim 2:15 as a genitive of place rather than agency. In this case, the term *dia* refers to "difficult circumstances through which women must pass." The author of 1 Timothy is saying that women will be saved *despite* the pain they suffer from bearing children as long as they continue in "faith, love, holiness, and chastity." Coupland observes that it is therefore not childbearing or the pain of childbearing which saves, but "being in Christ."[40]

These interpretations all suppose that τεκνογονία, *teknogonia*, is a reference to the literal act of childbearing.[41] One of two conse-

---

38. Porter, "What Does It Mean," 102.

39. Kroeger and Kroeger, *I Suffer Not A Woman*, 177, 176.

40. Coupland, "Salvation through Childbearing?," 302–3. Coupland succinctly describes the legacy of difficulty that has been bequeathed to modern scholarship by our passage. "New Testament scholars have long been bewildered or bemused by the enigmatic remark in 1 Timothy 2:15. . . . This bewilderment is reflected by the marginal notes in some translations. . . . The theological problem posed by the verse is obvious. How could the author . . . suggest that salvation could come not through faith in Christ alone, but through the 'work' of childbearing?" Furthermore, Coupland is correct that previous christological, physiological, and traditional interpretations of the remark are inconsistent with Pauline and "Deutero-Pauline" thought.

41. As also supposed by Dibelius and Conzelmann, *The Pastoral Epistles*, 49. For them, the author of 1 Timothy is here advocating preservation of the natural order against "syncretistic and ascetic tendencies and movements." Literal childbearing is also here supposed by Johnson, *The First and Second*

quences result: either a wedge is driven between "childbearing" and salvation for women so that the one does not really have anything to do with the other, or salvation for women is made dependent upon childbearing literally understood.[42] Both options pose a problem in the context of 1 Timothy. The author does indeed appear to connect the salvation of women to childbearing, but the idea is at odds with the rest of Pauline thought when it is taken literally.

A better solution to the problem of salvation of women through childbearing appears when we extend Padgett's and Perriman's metaphorical interpretations to include the reference to "childbearing." There is more here than a symbolic use of Adam and Eve; there is a non-literal use of the image of childbearing as well. In other words, the whole of 1 Tim 2:11–15 is non-literal or metaphorical. As we shall argue, the term "childbearing" refers only to birthing the virtues of faith, love, holiness, and temperance.[43] We therefore see a *postnatal* relationship between the four virtues

---

Letter to Timothy, 207–8; Schreiner, "An Interpretation of 1 Timothy 2:9–15," 150–51; Collins, *I & II Timothy and Titus*, 76, who says that "The Pastor reaffirms the traditional maternal role of women."

42. It is clear that the author's statement in 1 Tim 2:15 is an answer to the problem of Eve's transgression (παράβασις, *parabasis*) mentioned in 1 Tim 2:14. Despite the echo of Gen 3:16, there is no evidence at all that he or his audience is concerned about the pain women feel when giving birth. The central question is, How will the transgressor "Eve" be saved? The answer is, "through childbearing." Narrative flow and context leaves us little choice but to read the prepositional object of διά, *dia*, as a genitive of agency, contrary to Coupland.

43. In Prov 8:32–36, we have the converse idea. Instead of humans giving birth to virtues, it is the virtue wisdom (חכמה, σοφία; *hkmh, sophia*) that has given birth to humans. Also, in Philo, *Conf.* 49, wisdom is the mother of the wise. However, in Philo, *Fug.* 50–52, Bethuel is the father of Rebekah, yet his name means "the daughter of God," an appellation for wisdom. Philo asks, "How can wisdom, the daughter of God, be called a father?" Philo explains that even though wisdom is the daughter of God, it is both male and a father in that it sows the seeds of learning, education, knowledge, prudence, and *begats* (γεννῶντα, *gennōnta*) in the soul "good and praiseworthy practices." See also *Corp. herm.* 13.2, where Hermes Trismegisthus explains the doctrine of spiritual rebirth. Tat, his son and pupil complains, "I do not know from what womb a human being is born again, nor from what seed." Hermes responds, "O son, Wisdom is the womb which gives birth in silence, and the seed is the true Good."

of 2:15 and those women of Ephesus who will be saved. We shall contend that there was nothing strange about this use of the term τεκνογονία, *teknogonia*, in the world of the author and audience of 1 Timothy.

In 1 Tim 2:15, the key phrase includes a genitive construction with the generic article (σωθήσεται δὲ διὰ τῆς τεκνογονίας, *sōthēsetai de dia tēs teknogonias*), lit. "Yet she will be saved through *the* childbearing." The use of the generic article is characteristic of the author of 1 Timothy, for example, "fight the good fight of *faith* (τῆς πίστεως, *tēs pisteōs*), take hold of *eternal life* (τῆς αἰωνίου ζωῆς, *tēs aiōniou zōēs*)" (6:12).[44] The terms in this verse could be translated "*the* faith" and "*the* eternal life," but it is not necessary to translate the generic article at all. It has categorizing, but no particularizing force.[45] In English translation, the generic article may be omitted to avoid awkward syntax. Nevertheless, there are those who argue, on the basis of the article in 1 Tim 2:15, that the author speaks of women being saved through birth of *the child* (i.e., the Christ child). First, this argument turns the generic article into a particular article.[46] Second, it turns 2:15 into a Christological statement. There is nothing in the passage nor its context that justifies either maneuver. Those who make this argument are simply reading too much into the article. The use of the article only denotes τεκνογονία, *teknogonia* as a class of childbearing distinct from the birthing of literal children.

Nevertheless, there should be some engagement with a representative of the Christological interpretation of 1 Tim 2:15. Jared August introduces his essay on 1 Tim 2:15 saying, "Despite the diversity of views, this essay proposes that τῆς τεκνογονίας should be viewed as a reference to a specific childbirth—not to childbearing in general—and therefore that Paul intended a messianic understanding of this passage."[47] For August, the evidence for this insight is the

---

44. The generic article appears in 1 Tim 1:1, 5, 11, 14; 2:3, 15; 3:9, 16; 4:1, 6, 8, 12; 6:5, 12; 2 Tim 2:10, 15; 3:15; 4:3, 8; Titus 3:5.

45. See Smyth (*Greek Grammar*, 287), who says, "The generic article denotes an entire class as distinguished from other classes."

46. Smyth (*Greek Grammar*, 287), describes the particular article.

47. August, "What Must She Do To Be Saved?," 84–85.

Adam/Christ contrast that appears in the NT background (Luke 3:38; Rom 5:14; 1 Cor 15:22, 45; Jude 14). According to August, this is a pattern that also appears in 1 Tim 2:13–15. In all these places, Adam's sin and failure is overcome by the victory of Christ. By recalling the story of Adam and Eve, Paul calls attention to "God's creation design" in Genesis.[48] The text of 1 Tim 2:15 focuses specifically upon Eve who will be saved through the birth of a specific child, the Messiah. August maintains that this is consistent with the use of the singular verb form for future salvation. Moreover, Paul's use of the article (τῆς, *tēs*) is consistent with the OT expectation of a specific childbirth.[49]

Contrary to August, I would point out that there is indeed a shift in focus from Adam to Eve in 2:14–15, although August struggles to keep the focus on both Adam and Eve. For August, it is both Adam and Eve ("they") who must continue in faith, love, and holiness with self-control. However, aside from the disappearance of Adam from 2:15, this goes against August's own contention that Eve is the specific focus of 2:15.[50] Another problem is that the contrast in 2:13–15 is explicitly between Adam and Eve, not Adam and Christ. August feels that he has detected an Adam/Christ pattern in 1 Tim 2:13–15, yet unlike the other Scriptures (Romans and 1 Corinthians), where this pattern appears, there is no explicit mention of Christ in 2:13–15. That makes it very doubtful that this pattern actually extends to 2:13–15.[51] August would maintain that Christ is implied in the mention of childbirth, but again this goes against the pattern. In the Adam/Christ dichotomy, it is the death and resurrection of Christ, not his birth, that redeems and saves (Rom 5:10, 18; 1 Cor 15:21–22). Above all, as I have indicated, the author's characteristic use of the generic article is the more relevant pattern that includes 2:15. Therefore, *the birth of the child* is not in view in 1 Tim 2:15. It is the birth of virtues that is indicated.

---

48. August, "What Must She Do To Be Saved?," 85–86, 93.
49. August, "What Must She Do To Be Saved?," 89–90.
50. August, "What Must She Do To Be Saved?," 87, 90–91.
51. I also doubt that the pattern appears in Luke 3:38 and Jude 14.

2

Exploring the background
The World of Timothy and Paul

VIRTUES AS CHILDREN IN GNOSTICISM AND GREEK MYTHOLOGY

The idea of virtues *and vices* as children is a commonplace in the Gnostic literature of a later period. In *Orig. World*, 106–7, for example, the vices are *begotton* by the archon Death:

> Then Death, being androgynous, mingled with his (own) nature and begot seven androgynous offspring. These are the names of the male ones: Jealousy, Wrath, Tears, Sighing, Suffering, Lamentation, Bitter Weeping. And these are the names of the female ones: Wrath, Pain, Lust, Sighing, Curse, Bitterness, Quarrelsomeness. They had intercourse with one another, and each one begot seven, so that they amount to forty-nine androgynous demons.[1]

On the other hand, the virtues are *created* by the archon Zoe:

> And in the presence of these, Zoe, who was with Sabaoth, created seven good androgynous forces. These are the names of the male ones: the Unenvious, the Blessed,

1. Bethge and Layton, "On the Origin of the World," 177.

the Joyful, the True, the Unbegrudging, the Beloved, the Trustworthy. Also, as regards the female ones, these are their names: Peace, Gladness, Rejoicing, Blessedness, Truth, Love, Faith (Pistis). And from these there are many good and innocent spirits.[2]

Given the parallelism between these two acts of generation, and the characteristic "birthing" theme in Gnostic texts, there is no reason to think that the *creation* of these virtues by Zoe occur by some means other than birthing. In these two cases, however, the vices and virtues are children of archonic beings and are themselves hypostatized into archonic beings.

The idea of birthing *vices* recurs in *Paraph. Shem* 23:30 where it is said of the wind demons that "they gave birth to all kinds of unchastity."[3] The idea of birthing *virtues* recurs in *Exeg. Soul* 134:30 saying, "Thus when the soul [had adorned] herself again in her beauty . . . enjoyed her beloved, and [he also] loved her. . . . [S]o that by him she bears good children and rears them."[4] In context, "bearing and rearing good children" benefits the soul with "her rejuvenation," "resurrection from the dead," "ascent to heaven," "being born again," and "salvation" (*Exeg. Soul* 134:30). The children of the soul in this context can only be virtues. *The Exegesis of the Soul* 134:30 is a striking, although remote, thematic parallel to 1 Tim 2:15.

Even though this language represents a late stage of development in Gnostic thought, it is reasonable to presume that the *Gnostic* idea of virtues and vices as children had at least an inchoate form in the environment of 1 Timothy. This is especially so if there was an inchoate form of Gnosticism in the environment of 1 Timothy as 1 Tim 6:20, with its reference to "what is falsely called *gnōseōs* (γνώσεως)" would seem to indicate.

However, one need not look only to Gnosticism to find the idea of virtues and vices as children. In Greek mythology, the virtues *Diké*, *Eirene*, and *Eunomia* (Δίκη, Εἰρήνη, and Εὐνομία, Justice, Peace, and Order) along with *Horae* (Ὧραι, Hours) were the daughters

---

2. Bethge and Layton, "On the Origin of the World," 177.
3. Wisse, "The Paraphrase of Shem," 351.
4. Robinson and Scopello, "The Exegesis of the Soul," 196.

of the chief god Zeus and the titanide Themis.[5] Furthermore, the Three Graces-*Euphrosyne, Aglaia,* and *Thalia* (Εὐφροσύνη, Ἀγλαΐα, and Θαλία, Merriment, Beauty, and Cheerfulness) were the daughters of Zeus and the titanide *Eurynome* (Hesiod, *Theog.* 909, 945).[6] One cannot help but be struck by the formal similarity between the terms *Euphrosyne* and *sophrosynē* (σωφροσύνη, 1 Tim 2:15).[7] We also find fourteen vices and other negative entities which were the children of the goddess Strife (Ἔρις, *Eris*), namely, Toil, Forgetfulness, Famine, Sorrows, Fightings, Battles, Murders, Manslaughters, Quarrels, Lying Words, Disputes, Lawlessness, Ruin, and Oath (*Theog.* 224-32).[8]

Whether influenced directly by Gnosticism or not, the audience of 1 Timothy, as acculturated Hellenes, would have been familiar with the idea of virtues and vices as children.[9] Most likely, the audience of 1 Timothy would have automatically read the meaning of virtues as children into the author's use of τεκνογονία, *teknogonia*. Such a reading would have been a natural, although metaphorical, interpretation of good works (ἔργα ἀγαθά, *erga agatha*) for women in 1 Tim 2:10. Oddly, *we* probably would have been spared years of modern exegetical difficulty if the author of 1 Timothy had used

---

5. In *Theog.* 218-19. Zeus and Themis were also the progenitors of the Three Fates—Clotho, Lachesis, and Atropos. See also *Theog.* 76-79 where Zeus and Mnemosyne are the progenitors of the Nine Muses—Cleio, Euterpe, Thaleia, Melpomena, Terpsichore, Erato, Polyhymnia, Urania, and Calliope. All anglicized spellings of names in the *Theogony* are from the Loeb translation by Evelyn-White.

6. Cf. Philo, *Somn.* 2.174 on *euphrosyne,* and *Abr.* 54 on the three graces.

7. The term εὔφρων, *euphrōn*, a root of εὐφροσύνη, *euphrosynē*, means "sound mind, reasonable," which is very close to the meaning of σωφροσύνη, *sophrosynē*, "temperance, sound-mindedness."

8. The sire of these entities, if there was one, is not named. Strife herself was the daughter of Night (Νύξ, *Nyx*).

9. See Young, *The Theology of the Pastoral Letters,* 20-21. Concerning the Pastoral Epistles, Young says, "The Christian communities for which these epistles were intended are certainly to be located in a Hellenistic urban setting. Far more than in the authentic Paulines the vocabulary and allusions betray the assumptions of such a world." Young further observes, "On the other hand, these letters are pervaded by a religious culture that must stem from Hellenistic Judaism."

the term "fruit bearing" instead of "childbearing" in 2:15.[10] If the author had used the agricultural rather than the more appropriate gynecological metaphor, the postnatal or post-generative relationship between the four virtues and the women in 2:15 would probably have been more readily recognized by modern interpreters.[11] However, we should not suppose that the congregation of Timothy would have had the same difficulties grasping the gynecological metaphor that we seem to have had. After all, women are not fruit trees. Women give birth to children, not fruit. It would then make good cultural sense to speak of metaphorical "Eves" giving birth to metaphorical children. As we shall see, the most prevalent metaphorical use of children in the cultural environment of the Pastoral Epistles was as references to virtues. The author of 1 Timothy therefore uses his audience's familiarity with a commonplace idea to introduce a more Christian form of that same idea.

Incidentally, in Gal 4:19, Paul declares that he is in birth-pangs (ὠδίνω, ōdinō) for his children (i.e., "my children," τέκνα μου, tekna mou) until Christ is formed (μορφωθῇ Χριστός, morphōthē Christos) in them.[12] This is not the same idea as Ephesian women giving birth to virtues in 1 Tim 2:15. Still this verse helps to make a point

10. In the Gnostic tractate, *Apoc. Adam* 6.1, a remnant of the descendants of Noah are referred to as "fruit-bearing trees." Cf. Odes Sol 11:16a-21 where the inhabitants of Paradise are referred to as "blooming and fruit-bearing trees" (Charlesworth, "Odes of Solomon," 745). See also *Pss Sol* 14:2-5 where the Lord's "devout ones" are referred to as "the trees of life" (Wright, "Psalms of Solomon," 663). See MacRae, "Apocalypse of Adam," 715n6c. In *Ebr.* 8, Philo speaks of "virtue and vice" as "neither blossoming nor bearing fruit at the same time." In Philo, *Congr.* 40 Ephraim represents memory but his name means "fruit-bearing" because "the soul of the man who remembers bear as fruit the very things he has learned and loses none of them" (Cf. Philo, *Mut.* 98–100; *Sobr.* 28; *Migr.* 205). Particularly in Philo, *Gig.* 4 and *Plant.* 132, 136 the metaphors "children" and "fruit" are used interchangeably. Again, in *L.A.B.* 42.1-3—the story of Manoah and Eluma, the parents of Samson—the terms "children" and "fruit" are used interchangeably (Harrington, *Pseudo-Philo*, OTP, 355).

11. This may be primarily because of the influence of Matt 7:16–20; 12:33; Gal 5:22-26 on Western thinking.

12. Cf. Phlm 10 where Paul the Apostle speaks of Onesimus as "*my child* [ἐμοῦ τέκνου, emou teknou], to whom I *gave birth* [ἐγέννησα, egennēsa] while I was imprisoned."

about the distance between the perspective of ancient writers and our modern sensibilities. If the idea of Ephesian women giving birth to virtues is strange to modern hearers, then it is certainly no stranger than the idea of the male Paul giving birth to Galatian believers who are themselves pregnant with Christ.[13]

VIRTUES AS CHILDREN IN PHILO

Most strikingly, the idea of virtues as children appear in the allegorizing interpretations of Philo.[14] We have already referred to Philo's allegorical interpretation of the story of the Hebrew midwives as soul giving birth to virtue (*Leg.* 3.3), an idea not far from that of a pure heart issuing in virtue in 1 Tim 1:5 (cf. 1 Tim 1:19; 2 Tim 2:22). We have also already referred to Philo's allegorical understanding of the children of Noah as virtues, an understanding similarly implied in 1 Tim 2:15 for the children of the Ephesian women, and similarly made more explicit by context.

Philo interprets other narratives from the Hebrew Scriptures in the same metaphorical way, even to the point of allegorical rewording of patriarchal statements. In *Leg.* 3.180-81, Jacob responds to Rachel's request for children saying,

---

13. One might make a remote comparison to a somewhat converse idea in Plato's *Resp.* 6.496A where the sophisms of incompetent male philosophers are likened to "illegitimate and base children" (γεννᾶν νόθα καὶ φαῦλα, *gennan notha kai phaula*).

14. In *Congr.* 43-44, in his midrash on 1 Chr 7:14 and Gen 11:29, Philo explains his allegorical method: "Let no one in his right mind suppose that the wise lawgiver wrote these things as a historical record [ἱστορικὴ γενεαλογία, *historikē genealogia*], for these are matters of the soul [πραγμάτων ψυχήν, *pragmatōn psychēn*] which can be explained only through symbolic interpretation [συμβόλων ἀνάπτυξις, *symbolōn anaptyxis*]. When the things named are translated into our own language then we shall know their underlying truth." Cf. *Congr.* 180. Philo refers to allegorical, figurative, metaphorical, or symbolic interpretation numerous times in *Her.* 50; *Deus* 95; *Fug.* 181; *Somn.* 2.207, 260; *Abr.* 99, 131, 147; *Spec* 1.327; 2.29; *Prob.* 82; *QG* 1.52; 2.36, 37; 3.24, 25, 32; *Opif.* 154-55; *Cher.* 1.21, 25; *Det.* 167; *Post.* 100; *Migr.* 203; *Agr.* 97, 157; *Plant.* 36.

Exploring the Background

You have greatly erred, because I am not in the place of God, who alone is able to open *the wombs of souls* [τὰς ψυχῶν μήτρας, *tas psychōn mētras*], and sow virtues [ἀρετάς, *aretas*] in them, and make them to be pregnant [ποιεῖν ἐγκύμονας, *poiein enkymonas*] and to give birth to good things [τικτούσας τὰ καλά, *tiktousas ta kala*].[15]

Elsewhere, Philo interprets Sarah's birthing of Isaac in terms of virtue (ἀρετῇ, *aretē*) giving birth (τέτοκεν, *tetoken*) to happiness (εὐδαιμονία, *eudaimonia*), that is, as virtue giving birth to virtue (*Leg.* 2.82). Philo affirms the birth of virtue even while condemning that which is antithetical to virtue. In *Leg.* 3.68, God curses the serpent, which represents Pleasure (ἡδονή, *hēdonē*) because "she does *not possess in the womb* [οὐκ ἐχούσῃ, *ouk echousē*] any seed of virtue, but is always and everywhere full of guilt and pollution."

Sarah returns as "the virtue that rules over my soul" in *Congr.* 6. She "bears children without the aid of a midwife" (ὡς μηδὲ μαιευτικῆς τέχνης, *hōs mēde maieutikēs technēs*). Those children (τὰ γεννήματα, *ta gennēmata*) are identified as "the practice of prudence, the practice of justice, and the practice of piety" (τὸ φρονεῖν, τὸ δικαιοπραγεῖν, καὶ τὸ εὐσεβεῖν, *to phronein, to dikaiopragein, kai to eusebein*). Earlier in this same context her children are identified as "honorable words, irreproachable counsels, and praiseworthy practices" (λόγους δὲ ἀστείους καὶ βουλὰς ἀνεπιλήπτους καὶ ἐπαινετὰς πράξεις, *logous de asteious kai boulas anepilēptous kai epainetas praxeis*) (*Congr.* 4). Philo draws a contrast between Sarah's children and the many vices of his own youth. He describes these vices as the "multitude of *illegitimate children* [νόθων παίδων, *nothōn paidōn*] which were *born in* [ἀπεκύησαν, *apekyēsan*] me through vain imaginations [κεναὶ δόξαι, *kenai doxai*]." Sarah's children, on the other hand, are "the firstfruits" (τὰς ἀπαρχάς, *tas aparchas*) rendered back to God who "opened her womb" (μήτραν ἀνοιξαντι, *mētran anoixanti*)(cf. *Congr.* 98; *Mut.* 77–79; *Abr.* 99).

In *Congr.* 13–23, Hagar, the handmaiden of Sarah, represents "education" (παιδεία, *paideia*) or "the middle education of the intermediate and encyclical branches of knowledge" (τὴν τῶν μέσων καὶ

---

15. Cf. *Leg.* 2.82; *Cher.* 2.45–52.

ἐγκυκλιων ἐπιστημῶν μέσην παιδείαν, *tēn tōn meson kai enkyklion epistēmōn mesēn paideian*). Her children then are "abundant learning and intelligence" (πολυμάθειαν καὶ καταφρονητικῶς, *polymatheian kai kataphronētikōs*). As Abraham did not have a child by Sarah until after he had a child by Hagar, so the human soul cannot *produce the offspring* (τεκνοποιήσῃ, *teknopoiēsē*) of virtue until it has produced the offspring of education.

In *Her.* 50, Leah represents that case "when the soul is *pregnant and begins to give birth* [κυοφορῇ καὶ τίκτειν ἄρχηται, *kyophorē kai tiktein archētai*] to that which is proper for the soul," while Rachel represents "all that of the senses which is barren and *incapable of bearing children* [ἀτοκεῖ, *atokei*]" (cf. *Mut.* 132–33; *Plant.* 134–37).

In *Leg.* 3.88–89, Rebekah is "the soul that waits on God." When God tells her that "two nations are in your womb" the meaning is that the soul contains both "that which is base and irrational" (τὸ φαῦλον καὶ ἄλογον, *to phaulon kai alogon*) and "that which is honorable and rational and better" (τὸ ἀστεῖον καὶ λογικὸν καὶ ἄμεινον, *to asteion kai logikon kai ameinon*). The birth of Esau and Jacob therefore represents the soul giving birth respectively to vice and virtue (Cf. *Congr.* 129; *Sacri.* 4).

In Philo's allegory of Adam and Eve, Adam represents Mind (νόος, *noos*) while Eve represents "sense-perception" (αἴσθησις, *aisthēsis*). Each one bears "offspring" (ἔκγονα, *ekgona*), "the offspring of the Mind being the things of mind (τὰ νοητά, *ta noēta*), and the offspring of sense-perception being the things of the senses (τὰ αἰσθητά, *ta aisthēta*)" (*Leg.* 3.198; cf. *QG* 1.37; *Cher* 2.60). Philo interprets God's word to Eve, "In sorrow you shall bring forth children" (ἐν λύπαις τέξῃ τέκνα, *en lypais texē tekna*) (Gen 3:16) to mean that sense produces perception with great pain, especially for the foolish (*Leg.* 3.216; cf. *Leg.* 1.75). But when God says in Gen 3:16, "And you shall take refuge in your husband" (καὶ πρὸς τὸν ἄνδρα σου ἡ ἀποστροφή σου, *kai pros ton andra sou hē apostrophē sou*), the meaning is that sense has two husbands, Mind and Pleasure, "the one lawful, and the other an *abortioner*" (ὁ μὲν νόμιμος, ὁ δὲ φθορεύς, *ho men nomimos, ho de phthoreus*) (*Leg.* 3.220).[16]

---

16. Cf. "the one lawful, the other a seducer" (Colson and Whitaker, *Philo*, 451) and "The one a legal one, the other a destroyer" (Yonge, *Works of Philo*, 75).

But when sense turns to Mind, "her lawful husband" (τὸν νόμιμον ἄνδρα, *ton nomimon andra*) then "there are great benefits" (μεγίστη ἐστὶν ὠφέλεια, *megistē estin ōheleia*) (*Leg*. 3.221). In the context of Philo's thought, these "great benefits" are nothing less than the birth of virtue, such as occurred when Sarah (virtue) gave birth to Isaac (happiness) (*Leg*. 3.217).

Philo, when considered together with Greek mythology, further shows that the idea of virtues and vices (ἀρετὰς καὶ κακίας, *aretas kai kakias*) as children was not peculiar to strictly Gnostic or proto-Gnostic thought. It was a feature of Hellenistic thinking generally speaking. More importantly, Philo shows that the idea of virtues and vices as children of the soul occurred in the context of biblical exegesis of the Genesis narrative (e.g., *Leg*. 3.246–47) and was in currency at the time of 1 Timothy and before.[17] It is also of great relevance that it is not gods, goddesses, or archons that give birth to the virtues in Philo's midrash, but mostly the human heroines of Israel's history—Eve, Sarah, Hagar, Rebekah, Leah, Rachel, and the enslaved Hebrew women of Egypt.[18] Furthermore, in Philo the virtues themselves are not hypostatized into gods, goddesses, or archons, but remain the inward dispositions and *outward expressions* of the soul.[19] There is then both precedent and background for the listing of faith, love, holiness, and temperance as the products of "childbearing" by earthly women in 1 Tim 2:11–15.

Philo continues to rehearse the theme of virtues as children when he leaves the Hebrew Scriptures to give an historical account of a cenobitic Egyptian community known as the *Therapeutae*. The women of this community are called *Therapeutrides* (*Contempl*. 2). He particularly speaks of the *Therapeutrides* as participants in a Pentecost forefeast and also as mothers of virtues:

17. Philo also interprets "children" as a metaphorical reference to the senses, i.e., sight, hearing, smelling, and feeling (*QG* 1.49).

18. However, in *Ebr*. 165, the daughters of Lot themselves are allegorized as Counsel (βουλή, *boulē*) and Assent (συναίνεσις, *synainesis*).

19. Augustine (354–430 CE) will later criticize the Roman practice of hypostatizing virtues and vices into divine or semi-divine beings in *Civ*. 4.20–24. Pseudo-Phocylides had much earlier rejected the Greek practice of making a god out of *eros*, which he instead characterized as a dangerous vice (*Ps-Phoc*. 194).

Women, Salvation, and Childbearing

> And the women also share in this feast, the greater part of whom, though old, are virgins in respect of their purity (not indeed through necessity, as some of the priestesses among the Greeks are, who have been compelled to preserve their chastity more than they would have done of their own accord), but out of an admiration for and love of wisdom, with which they are desirous to pass their lives, on account of which they are indifferent to the pleasures of the body, *desiring not mortal but immortal children* [οὐ θνητῷ ἐκγόνων ἀλλ' ἀθανάτων, *ou thnētō ekgonōn all' athanatōn*], which *the soul that is attached to God is alone able to birth by itself and from itself* [ἃ μόνη τίκτειν ἀφ' ἑαυτῆς οἷα τέ ἐστιν ἡ θεοφιλὴς ψυχή, *ha monē tiktein aph' eautēs hoi te estin hē theophilēs psychē*], the Father having sown in it rays of light appreciable only by the intellect, by means of which it will be able to perceive the doctrines of wisdom. (*Contempl.* 68)[20]

Notably, in Philo, we see how a discussion of women *attracts* the metaphor of childbearing (rather than fruit bearing) as an expression for producing virtues. A discussion of women also attracts the metaphor of childbearing in 1 Tim 2:15. This is made more opportune by the reference to literal childbearing in Gen 3:16.

VIRTUES AS CHILDREN IN PLATO

The idea of the human soul *giving birth* to virtues or vices is characteristically Platonic. In *Symp.* 206C, Diotima, the wise woman of Mantineia, declares, "All people are pregnant (κυοῦσι, *kyousi*), Socrates, both in body and soul."[21] Again, in *Symp*, virtues born of the soul are specifically referred to as *children* in contrast to human children literally understood. As Diotima says to Socrates concerning the Athenian statesman, Solon, and other benefactors:

---

20. Adapted from Yonge, *The Works of Philo*, 704.

21. In *Congr.* 129, Philo refers to "souls which are pregnant with wisdom" and ready to "bring forth children." The same idea is found in *QG* 3.10: "For every rational soul bears good fruit or is fruitful" (Marcus, *Philo*, 194). In *Det.* 127, "the mind becomes pregnant and labors to give birth to the things of mind." In *Migr.* 140, Sarah represents "the soul that appears to be pregnant."

Exploring the Background

And Solon is honored among you because *he gave birth to the laws* [τὴν τῶν νόμων γέννησιν, *tēn tōn nomōn gennēsin*], and so are many other men in many other places, among both Hellenes and barbarians, who performed many good works, and *gave birth to a multitude of virtues* [γεννήσαντες παντοίαν ἀρετήν, *gennēsantes pantoian aretē*]. In their names many shrines have been built because *they had such children* [γέγονε διὰ τοὺς τοιούτους παῖδας, *gegone dia tous toioutous paidas*], but none of them has been so honored for having *human children* [διὰ τοὺς ἀνθρωπίνους, *dia tous anthrōpinous*]. (*Symp.* 209D–E)

In this same context, Diotima explains to Socrates that those who are "pregnant in their souls ... further *conceive and bear ... wisdom and the other virtues*" (ἄ ψυχῇ προσήκει καὶ κυῆσαι καὶ τεκεῖν ... φρόνησίν τε καὶ τὴν ἄλλην ἀρετήν, *ha psychē prosēkei kai kyēsai kai tekein ... phronēsin te kai tēn allēn aretēn*) and "everyone would prefer *to have such children born to him rather than human children*" (καὶ πᾶς ἄν δέξαιτο ἑαυτῷ τοιούτους παῖδας μᾶλλον γεγονέναι ἤ τοὺς ἀνθρωπίνους, *kai pas an dexaito eautō toioutous paidas mallon gegonenai ē tous anthrōpinous*) (*Symp.* 209A–D).[22]

In Plato then, we find a *natalistic* concept of virtue. Virtues are birthed by the soul just as children are birthed by women. Accordingly, the soul is referred to as "she" (αὐτή, *autē*) in Platonic thought regardless of whether the soul resides in the body of a male or female.[23] As Socrates questions Cebes, "Whatever the soul occupies, *she* always comes to it bringing life?" He questions again, "Then soul will never receive the opposite to that which *she* brings?"

---

22. Of course, the context of Plato's narrative in this case is the celebration of pederastic relationships in which communion between an older male teacher and a younger male pupil results in "a much greater fellowship than those who have children together" (*Symp.* 209C). Aristotle, Philo, and Paul would have condemned such a relationship (see Aristotle, *Eth. nic.* 7.5.3; 7.7.7; Philo, *Spec.* 3.39; Rom 1:26–27; 1 Cor 6:9; cf. 1 Tim 1:10). Also see Philo, *Contempl.* 57–61 for his scathing critique of this aspect of Plato's *Symposium*.

23. Philo refers to the soul as mother and nurse (μήτηρ καὶ τροφός, *mētēr kai trophos*) (*Somn.* 2.139). Philo also speaks of "the womb of the soul" (τῆς ψυχῆς μήτρας, *tēs psychēs mētras*) (*Migr.* 34) without regard to the gender of the body.

WOMEN, SALVATION, AND CHILDBEARING

(*Phaed.* 105D; cf. 106B, 107C).[24] As we have seen, in Philo we have both a *natalistic* and *generative* concept of virtue, that is to say, a use of both the gynecological and agricultural reproductive metaphors.[25] Both concepts and metaphors express the same Platonic idea in Philo.

A contrasting view is provided by Aristotle.[26] In the *Nicomachean Ethics*, Aristotle argues for an *active* or *kinetic* concept of virtue. Virtue is more what one does; it is not just what one gives birth to within the soul.[27] However, while Aristotle avoids natalistic language he is not altogether free of generative elements in this discourse about virtue. In *Eth. nic.* 4.3.33-34, Aristotle speaks of "the high-minded man" (μεγαλόψυχος, *megalopsychos*) as "one who would rather possess things that are good and *bear no fruit* [ἄκαρπα, *akarpa*], rather than things that are *fruit bearing* [καρπίμων, *karpimōn*] and cause others to be obligated to him; for in this way he would retain his autonomy."[28]

There is no question about Plato's influence upon Philo and the Gnostics, particularly in regard to the idea of virtues as children.[29] Plato himself was most likely influenced in this regard by

---

24. The English translation is from Rouse, *Plato*, 584. Rouse's translation preserves the feminine pronoun, unlike those of Fowler, *Plato*, 363-64, and Grube, *Pheado*, 90-91.

25. Even in Philo, *Deus* 117-18, where it is Noah who gives birth to virtues, the metaphor is still gynecological, because it is not really Noah, but his soul that gives birth. In a large part of Hellenistic thought, the soul is female.

26. In *Somn.* 1.167-68, Philo seems to take a mediating stance between the Platonic and Aristotelian schools in the debate over whether virtue comes by nature, practice, or learning. In *Abr.* 52, Abraham, Isaac, and Jacob respectively represent all three means of acquiring virtue (cf. Philo, *Ios.* 1).

27. See. Aristotle, *Eth. nic.* 6.13.1-8, Aristotle acknowledges that virtues may be innate qualities, that is to say, present in us at birth, but we only recognize them as virtues when they take the form of action; and in order for them to *properly* take the form of action, they must be governed by reason.

28. See Apostle, *Aristotle's Nicomachean Ethics*, 69. Apostle's translation preserves the agricultural reproductive metaphor, unlike Rackham's in the Loeb edition.

29. Plato's influence is pervasive in the Gnostic texts, but more specifically indicated in places like Plato Rep. 588A-589B in *NHL*, 318-20; and perhaps in *Exeg. Soul* 127, 134; *Teach. Silv.* 99; *Val. Exp.* 37, 39; *Tri. Trac.* 75-77; *Great*

the mythology of Homer and Hesiod among others.³⁰ Philo and the Gnostics also show direct influence by Homer and Hesiod among others.³¹ There are, however, no clear, unequivocal indications of direct influence by either Homer, Hesiod, Plato, or Philo anywhere in the Pauline corpus.³² Yet there is no denying of their influence in the Hellenistic world of the Pauline Epistles. Therefore, even if there is only an indirect influence, that influence is reflected in the natalistic or generative virtue language of the undisputed and disputed Pauline Epistles.³³

Pow. 43-44. The influence of Homer and Hesiod is also pervasive in the Gnostic texts, but probably more specifically indicated in the occurrences of names like Asclepius, Hades, Cerberus, Zeus, and Tartaros in *Asclepius* 21-29, 75; *Great Pow* 37, 41, 42; Plato Rep. 49; *Interp. Know* 13. However, in *Exeg. Soul* 136, 137, we have actual citations of the *Odyssey*.

30. He was at least influenced by Homer in regard to the use of natalistic language. In Plato, *Theaet.* 152E, Socrates dialogues with Theaetetus the mathematician about the ambivalent, transitory, flux-like character of reality as it is described in the philosophy of Heraclitus. Among others, he associates Homer with Heraclitus saying, "And when Homer spoke of 'Oceanus and Tethys, father and mother of the gods' [θεῶν γένεσιν καὶ μητέρα, *theōn genesin kai mētera*] he meant that all things were the *children of flux and motion* [ἔκγονα ῥοῆς τε καὶ κινήσεως, *ekgona rhēs te kai kinēseōs*]" (cf. Homer, *Il.* 14.201-2, 246). See also Plato, *Tim.* 40E-41A and *Crat.* 402B-C for more natalistic language involving Oceanus and Tethys. The influence of Homer and Hesiod upon Plato is indicated in *Crat.* 396B-C; 397E-398A; 402 B-C; *Lysis* 215C; *Min.* 318E-319D; *Menex* 238A; *Leg.* 2.658D and numerous other places in his writings.

31. E.g., Philo, *Aet.* 17, 18 (cf. Hesiod, *Theog.* 116). Here Philo reports that some people think that Hesiod was the "father" of Platonic thought. See also, *Aet.* 37 (cf. Homer, *Od.* 6.107); 132 (cf. Homer, *Il.* 6.147); *Migr.* 156 (cf. *Il* 6.484); 195 (cf. *Od* 4.392); *Contempl.* 40-41 (cf. *Od* 9.355); *Legat* 80 (cf. *Od* 4.363); and *QG* 3.3 (cf. *Od.* 12.183-94); 3.16 (cf. *Od* 14.258).

32. However, see the citations of Menander (343-292 BCE) in 1 Cor 15:33 and Epimenides (c. 600 BCE) in Titus 1:12. Cf. another citation possibly by Epimenides in Acts 17:28a, and one by Aratus (c. 315-240 BCE) or perhaps Cleanthes (c. 330-231 BCE) in Acts 17:28b. Note the natalistic language of this last citation. "For we are his offspring" (Τοῦ γὰρ καὶ γένος ἐσμέν, *Tou gar kai genos esmen*). Cf. Cleanthes, *Hymn to Zeus* 4, ἐκ σοῦ γὰρ γένος εἴσι, *ek sou gar genos eisi*.

33. After recounting a series of post-resurrection appearances of Christ, Paul says in 1 Cor 15:8, "Last of all, as one born before the time, he appeared to me also." Paul's reference to himself as "one born before the time"

Women, Salvation, and Childbearing

A more general mark of Hellenistic influence in the undisputed and disputed Pauline Epistles is the appearance of virtue and vice lists in this corpus.[34] First Timothy 2:15 is primarily a short virtue list similar to the short virtue lists that we find in Plato, *Resp.* 4.427E; *Lach.* 198B; *Prot.* 349B; Philo, *Prob* 70; *Post* 128; *Ebr.* 23; *Deus* 79; and Wis 8:7. Longer lists of virtues appear in Aristotle, *Eth. nic.* 2.2.7-9; 3.6.1-5.3.17; *Eth. eud.* 2.3.4; *Virt. vit.* 2.1-7; 4.1-5.7; 8.1-4; and Wis 7:22-23.[35] Short *vice* lists appear in Plato, *Resp.* 10.609B; Philo, *Conf.* 21; *Somn* 2.266; *Post* 52; 3 Bar 8:5 (Slavonic and Greek); and *T. Jud.* 16:1.[36] Longer vice lists appear in Aristotle, *Eth. nic.* 5.2.13; *Eth. eud.* 2.3.4; *Virt. vit.* 6.1-7.14; 3.1-8; Matt 15:19; 3 Bar 13:4 (Greek); Wis 14:25-26; and *T. Levi* 17:11. In Philo, *Sacri.* 32, there is an unusually *long* vice list, giving as many as 152 vices. Despite the variety, there is a discernible pattern of discourse in Hellenistic virtue ethics and the listing of virtues and vices seem to be the most notable aspect

---

(τῷ ἐκτρώματι; τὸ ἔκτρωμα, *tō ektrōmati; to ektrōma*) has been particularly troublesome to interpreters. Although there is still not enough evidence to be certain, this reference may be an allusion to Homer, *Il.* 19.118 where Hera causes the birth of Eurytheus "before the full course of months" (ἠλιτόμηνον ἐόντα, *ēlitomēnon eonta*). At the same time, Hera in her craftiness "held back the Eileithyiae" (σχέθε Εἰλειθυίας, *schethe Eileithyias*), the goddesses of childbirth, in order to delay the birth of Heracles against the wishes of unwary Zeus (*Il.* 19.119). Previously, Zeus had promised that the first of his descendants born on that day would become king of Argos (cf. Diodorus Siculus, *Bibl.hist.* 4.9.4). Paul may be saying that in the same way the prematurely born Eurytheus was made king over someone thought more deserving, he was made an apostle over others thought more deserving. Of course, Christ replaces Hera in this potential allegory of Paul as Eurysteus. For a survey of other interpretations, see Orr and Walther, *1 Corinthians*, 318, 322-23; Hollander and van der Hout, "The Apostle Paul Calling Himself an Abortion," 224-36; Mitchell, "Reexamining the 'Aborted Apostle,'" 469-85.

34. Virtue lists: Rom 5:3-5; 1 Cor 13:4-7; 2 Cor 6:6-7; Gal 5:22-23; Phil 4:8-9; Col 3:12-17; 1 Tim 2:15; 3:2-7, 8-10, 11-12; 6:11; 2 Tim 2:22; Titus 1:7-9; 2:2, 3-5, 6-8, 9-10, 11-12; 3:1-2. Vice lists: Rom 1:29-31; 13:13; 1 Cor 6:9; Gal 5:19-21; Col 3:8-9; 1 Tim 1:9-10; 2 Tim 3:2-5; Titus 3:3.

35. Aristotle, *Eth. eud.* 2.3.4 is actually a *mixed* list of both virtues and vices.

36. In *Conf.* 21, Philo describes the mind that is *pregnant* with evil. He refers to what may be called the four cardinal vices: folly, cowardice, intemperance, and injustice.

of that pattern.³⁷ Therefore, it is plain that the author of the Pastoral Epistles is familiar with at least this aspect of Hellenistic virtue ethics.³⁸ If this is the case, then we can hardly ignore the implications of his acquaintance with virtue and vice lists for our understanding of τεκνογονία, *teknogonia*, in 1 Tim 2:15.

VIRTUES AS CHILDREN IN JUDAISM

Questions about the virtues as children theme specifically *in Judaism* recur when we return to Philo's description of the *Therapeutrides* and their commitment to bearing *immortal children*. Is this language used by the *Therapeutae* themselves, or is Philo imposing his own Hellenized thought upon the community? If it is the former then we have more evidence of the theme in Diaspora Judaism. This is not to ignore Martin Hengel and restore an artificial wedge between Judaism and Hellenism; but it may be that the theme of virtues and vices as children found unique expression within Judaism.³⁹ Showing that this theme was incorporated into a Jewish heritage may not explain its attraction for the secondary audience of 1 Timothy (a Hellenized congregation of Christ-believers) but it may partially explain its significance for the author and his primary addressee (Timothy).

Since, Philo is so far our only independent witness to the Therapeutae, we have no basis for an autographic account of their language or rhetoric.⁴⁰ It is probably more likely that Philo imposes his own Hellenized view upon the Therapeutae.

---

37. The occurrence of domestic codes or *Haustafeln* in the Pauline corpus (Eph 5:22–6:4; Col 3:18–4:1; 1 Tim 3:4–5, 12; 6:1–2; Titus 2:9–10) is a related phenomenon and also a mark of Hellenistic influence. Cf. Martin, "The *Haustafeln*," 206–31; Donelson, *Colossians, Ephesians, 1 and 2 Timothy, and Titus*, 48–49, 131–33. Also, Aristotle, *Pol.* 1.12.

38. Orig. *World* 106–7 and *Theog.* 224–32 mentioned above are also forms of virtue and vice lists.

39. Hengel, *Judaism and Hellenism*, 58–106.

40. Pseudo-Dionysius (fifth–sixth century CE) in his *Eccl. hier.* 6.1–3, portrayed the Therapeutae as Christian monks. In any case, he appears to be dependent upon Philo. Campbell (*Dionysius the Pseudo-Areopagite*, 193n246)

Women, Salvation, and Childbearing

The Qumran community are, of course, the other cenobitic community often compared to the Therapeutae.[41] Although, pregnancy and birthing language occur frequently in the Dead Sea Scrolls, the idea of virtues as children does not seem to occur at all.[42] The closest we come to birthing virtues in the Dead Sea Scrolls is 4Q424. Fr. 3 where we hear that "a man of knowledge will *produce* wisdom" (איש ידע יפיק חכם, *'ysh yd' ypyq hkm*).[43] We are hard pressed to find anything more than this. In the Dead Sea Scrolls, human beings are usually the children of virtues or vices, rather than virtues or vices the children of human beings.[44]

Still, other occurrences of virtues and vices as children in the literature of Judaism may be enough to show that the theme had a respectable presence in Hebrew culture. We have a rare occurrence

---

says, "Considering the Neoplatonism of Dionysius and the absence of the term in other writings, it seems that he drew the term from the writings of Philo. Philo's treatise *De Vita Comtemplativa* is the description of a Jewish monastic sect called Therapeutae"

41. The 2007 Annual meeting of SBL, where this part of the study was first shared, featured an exhibit of the Dead Sea Scrolls at the San Diego Natural History Museum in Balboa Park. Presenters were encouraged to reference the Dead Sea Scrolls in their papers.

42. For pregnancy and birth language in the Dead Sea Scrolls note the following: "I was in distress like a woman giving birth first time when her birth-pangs come on her and a pain racks her womb to begin the birth in the <<crucible>> of the pregnant woman" (1QH10.7-9); "Resentment has taken hold of me and torments like the pangs of giving birth" (1QH13.30); "Since [pain] has gripped you [like a woman giving birth, have pain and push (it) out, daughter of Zion, like a woman giving birth](4Q168.1). See also 1QH20.8; 4Q427.2.7-8; 4Q429.4; These English translations are from García Martínez and Watson, *The Dead Sea Scrolls Translated*, 194, 331, 339, 355, 363, 368.

43. This involves a translation of פוק, *pwq* (bring out, furnish, promote, produce, elicit, obtain) that is supported by BDB. Cf. "a knowing man will bring forth wisdom" in Vermes, *The Complete Dead Sea Scrolls in English*, 415 and "The wise man will obtain Wisdom" in García Martínez and Watson, *The Dead Sea Scrolls Translated*, 394.

44. See "sons of justice" (4QSe 3.10; 4Q502.1-3.8); "sons of light" (1QM 1.11; 4Q511.10.4); "sons of darkness" (1QM3.6); "sons of your truth" (1QH17.35); "sons of his truth" (1QM17.8); "daughter of truth" (4Q502.1-3.6) in García Martínez and Watson *The Dead Sea Scrolls Translated*, 27, 95, 97, 112, 350, 373, 440.

Exploring the Background

in the Psalms where the wicked man gives birth to vices: "Behold, the wicked man conceives evil, and is pregnant with mischief, and gives birth to lies" (הנה יחבל-און והרה עמל ויֹלד שקר, *hnh yhbl-'wn whrh 'ml wyld shqr* (Ps 7:14).

Moreover, we have a striking occurrence in *Joseph and Aseneth*, where Repentance, a distinctively Jewish virtue (cf. Ezek 14:6; 18:30; Job 42:6; Matt 3:8; 9:13), is portrayed as the *daughter* of God and *sister* of the archangel Michael. On the occasion of her repentance and conversion, the archangel Michael tells the princess Aseneth:

> For Repentance [ἡ μετανοιά, *hē metanoia*] is in the heavens, an exceedingly beautiful and good *daughter of the Most High* [θυγάτηρ τοῦ ὑψίστου, *thygatēr tou hypsistou*]. And she herself entreats the Most High God for you at all times and for all who repent in the name of the Most High God, because he is (the) father of Repentance. And she herself is guardian and loves you very much, and is beseeching the Most High for you at all times and for all who repent she prepared a place of rest in the heavens. And she will renew all who repent, and wait on them herself for ever (and) ever. And Repentance is exceedingly beautiful, a virgin pure and laughing always, and she is gentle and meek. And therefore, the Most High Father loves her, and all the angels stand in awe of her. And I, too, love her exceedingly, because she is also my sister. And because she loves you virgins, I love you, too. (*Joseph and Aseneth* 15:7–8)[45]

In all of these cases we can hardly rule out Hellenistic influence; nevertheless, the theme of virtues and vices as children has been given a uniquely Jewish expression. Identifying these Jewish expressions only demonstrates the pervasiveness of the theme, although its pervasiveness in Judaism would bear little consequence for the formerly pagan Hellenes who constitute the audience of 1 Timothy.

---

45. Adapted from Burchard, "Joseph and Aseneth," 227. *Joseph and Aseneth* is dated first century BCE to second century CE.

3

Viewing the Landscape
Literature and Location

VIRTUES AS CHILDREN IN EARLY CHRISTIANITY

We also find a few more uniquely Christian expressions of the virtues as children theme as well, and these are distinct from those places in early Christian literature where the generation of virtues is described as "fruit bearing." In these cases, we actually have reference to "children" and "birth." They are significant because they show that 1 Tim 2:15 does not stand alone as an early Christian witness to the theme of the soul birthing virtues as if they were children.

In Luke 7:35, Jesus concludes his defense of himself and John with the words, "Yet wisdom is justified by all her children" (καὶ ἐδικαιώθη ἡ σοφία ἀπὸ πάντων τῶν τέκνων αὐτῆς, *kai edikaiōthē hē sophia apo pantōn tōn teknōn autēs*). It is customary in scholarship on this verse to identify the children of wisdom as Jesus and John themselves.[1] While this interpretation certainly has merit,

---

1. Gathercole, "The Justification of Wisdom," 476–88. Gathercole argues for Jesus and John as "children" or "envoys" of "Lady Wisdom" and particularly for Luke 7:35 as Jesus' bitter complaint against those who dissociate him and John from Wisdom's commissioning

a different one is almost demanded by the Matthean parallel and sensitivity to the theme of virtues as children.²

In Matthew 11:19, Jesus concludes, "Yet wisdom is justified by her works" (καὶ ἐδικαιώθη ἡ σοφία ἀπὸ πάντων τῶν ἔργων αὐτῆς, *kai edikaiōthē hē sophia apo pantōn tōn teknōn autēs kai edikaiō thē hē sophia apo pantōn tōn ergōn autēs*). The Lukan parallel therefore has "children" instead of "works" in a context where acts of temperance or self-control are ascribed to John, and acts of love or friendship are ascribed to Jesus. If it is better to understand "temperance" and "love" as the "works" of wisdom in the Matthean version, it would seem best to understand these virtues or *virtuous works* as the children of wisdom in the Lukan parallel. It is not Jesus and John then who are the children of wisdom in Luke, but the virtues that they show, that is to say, their respective virtues of love and temperance.

The idea of virtues giving birth to virtues is well attested in the wider literary context of the Gospels (Plato, *Resp.* 6.18 E; Philo, *Congr.* 6; *Leg.* 2.82; 3.217; cf. Philostratus, *Heroikos* 7.8). The idea of *mother wisdom* giving birth to virtues is particularly well attested (Philo, *Congr.* 129; *Fug.* 50–52; Prov 8:19; Wis 8:7; *Let. Aris.* 260; cf. Jas 3:17).

The *inter*textual transition from "her works" in Matt 11:19 to "all of her children" in Luke 7:35 seems to be paralleled by the *intra*textual transition from "good works" in 1 Tim 2:10 to "childbearing" in 1 Tim 2:15.

The terms "good works" and "childbearing" seem to be equivalent in meaning in 1 Timothy, but *not* as references to marrying, literally bearing children, child-rearing, homemaking, and other so-called "women's work." Rather both terms refers to virtues or virtuous works, namely, those designated by the terms faith, love, holiness, and temperance.³

---

2. Wisdom gives birth to human beings in Prov 8:32–36 and Philo, *Conf.* 49.

3. The occurrence of virtues as children in both the Gospel of Luke and the First Epistle to Timothy may once again raise the question of Luke as the author of the Pastoral Epistles. See Prior, "Revisiting the Pastoral Epistles," 2–19; Quinn and Wacker, *The First and Second Letters to Timothy*. However,

Women, Salvation, and Childbearing

As we have seen, both virtues and vices are conceived as children in ancient culture. In James 1:15 we have an early Christian expression of vice giving birth to vice. "Desire when it has conceived gives birth to sin; and sin when it is full-grown, gives birth to death" (εἶτα ἡ ἐπιθυμία συλλαβοῦσα τίκτει ἁμαρτίαν, ἡ δὲ ἁμαρτία ἀποτελεσθεῖσα ἀποκύει θάνατον, *eita hē epithymia syllabousa tiktei hamartian, hē de hamartia apotelestheisa apokyei thanaton*). It appears then that there is nothing unusual about the theme of virtue and vices as children in early Christianity, just as there is nothing unusual about this theme in the larger cultural world of early Christianity. *Moreover, both women and men are capable of pregnancy and childbearing in this sense.*

THE LEGACY OF IONIA AND ARTEMIS

Ephesus is the purported locale of Timothy and his congregation (1 Cor 16:8-11; 1 Tim 1:3; 2 Tim 1:18; 4:12). Even if this locale is a pseudepigraphal feature of the text—which is by no means an unassailable characterization—it is still significant that the author evokes an Ephesian provenance for the audience of the epistle.[4] Knowledgeable Hellenes among the readers of 1 Timothy would inevitably imagine a hearing of its author against the backdrop of Ephesian culture and all that is associated with it.[5] Ephesus is therefore a referent that evokes observations relevant to the present argument.

---

the sharing of this theme between the Gospel of Luke and 1 Timothy more likely indicates no more than a common Hellenistic influence.

4. While acknowledging the impossibility of demonstrating the authenticity of the Pastoral Epistles, Johnson nevertheless argues that the grounds for judging them inauthentic are so seriously flawed as to render these judgments invalid. After exploring the literary category of *mandata principis* (commandments of a ruler) as a possible genre for 1 Timothy and Titus, Johnson finds reason to seriously consider the provenance of 1 Timothy "not as a fictional setting, but perhaps as the real-life occasion for the letter." See Johnson, *The First and Second Letters to Timothy*, 91, 140-42.

5. See Arnold, "Ephesus," 249-52.

Viewing the Landscape

Ephesus was in that coastal province of West-Central Asia Minor and nearby islands known in earlier times as Ionia.[6] This region was the matrix for a widely influential and particular kind of philosophical thought. In time, this particular kind of philosophy was identified by the name of the region itself. It is not critical for our case that the audience of 1 Timothy have an actual provenance in the region of Ionia (although Ionia was the most likely provenance). It is significant enough that this audience is associated with that region in the minds of ancient readers.

The influence of Ionian philosophers and their legacy in the wider Greek world is an already well-rehearsed theme in classical studies.[7] Similarly, the prominence of Plato and Philo as heirs of Ionian thought is another commonplace.[8] Even though Ionian thought is a rationalization or "demythologizing" of Homer, Hesiod, and other epic lyricists, it retains some of the natalistic features of epic.[9] Ionian thought perpetuates the tradition of natalistic language.[10] The Ionian philosophers particularly drew upon the myth of the titans Oceanus and Tethys as "begetters" of all things, as a convenient source of metaphors and imagery (Aristotle, *Metaph.* 1.3.29-36; Plato, *Theat.* 152D-E; *Tim.* 40E-41A; *Crat.* 402B-C). Accordingly, Xenophanes says, "but the great ocean is begetter of

---

6. See Plato, *Thg.* 129D. Against Socrates' warning Sannio and Thrasyllus go on an expedition to "Ephesus and the rest of Ionia." Incidently, there are some scholarly doubts about the Platonic authorship of *Theages*.

7. See Schofield, "The Ionians," 47-83; Hall, "Ionians," 820-21; Waterfield, *The First Philosophers*, xi-xxxiii; Long, "The Scope of Early Greek Philosophy," 1-21.

8. See Peters, *The Harvest of Hellenism*, 300-308.

9. As founders of natural philosophy, the seventh-to-fifth century Ionian philosophers, Thales, Anaximander, Anaximenes, Anaxagoras, Empedocles, Pythagoras, Heraclitus, Democritus, Xenophanes, and others sought to replace mythological cosmologies with materialistic explanations for the universe. On the Ionian philosophers see Aristotle, *Metaph.* 1.3.19-1.5.28; 8.1.1-8.3.30; Augustine, *Civ.* 8.2; 18.37.

10. See Plato, *Resp.* 6.18E, where the Ideas are described as "the offspring of the good" (ἔκγονος τοῦ ἀγαθοῦ, *ekgonos tou agathou*). Also Plato, *Symp.* 203B-C where Eros (Ἔρως, Love) is lauded as the son of Poros (Πόρος, Resource) and Penia (Πενία, Poverty). See also Philostratus, *Heroikos* 7.8, where truth (ἀλήθεια, *alētheia*) is "the mother of virtue" (μητέρα ἀρετῆς, *mētera aretēs*).

clouds and winds and rivers."[11] Malcolm Schofield comments upon this statement of Xenophanes saying, "The striking description of the ocean (*pontos*) as 'begetter' already recalls, yet simultaneously rationalizes, Hesiod's account of how it 'begat' Nereus, the old man of the sea and other mythical figures (Theog 233-9)."[12] As rationalizers of myth, the Ionian philosophers were in large measure the founders of allegorical interpretation.[13]

Regardless of the actual place and destination of their literary compositions, it is this germinal Ionian heritage that binds Plato and Philo to Homer and Hesiod, and then binds them all to 1 Timothy at least in regard to the natalistic concept of virtue.[14] There is

---

11. Schofield, "The Ionians," 76. He identifies the source of this statement as "The Geneva Scholium on *Iliad* XXI." One might compare Job 38:29, where God asks Job, "From whose *womb* [MT: בטן, *btn*; LXX: γαστρός, *gastros*] does the ice come forth, and who has *given birth* [MT: ילד, *yld*; LXX: τέτοκεν, *tetoken*] to the hoarfrost of the heavens?" The implication is that it was God who conceived in the womb and gave birth to these phenomena. This is a rare and startling case of natalistic imagery applied to the God of Israel.

12. Schofield, "The Ionians," 76. Cf. also the reference to "men to whom the clouds gave birth" in *Apoc. Ab.* 14.6 (Rubinkiewicz and Lunt, "Apocalypse of Abraham," 696, especially note f).

13. See Peters, *The Harvest of Hellenism*, 451. "Plato, who cared only for the morality of the traditional myths as a criterion for their political use, reveals in passing that in his day there were those who saw an 'undersense' [*hyponoia*] in the myths. There is reason to suspect that this 'other reading' [*allegoria*] was being practiced by Anaxagoras and some of his disciples, and that the hidden meaning was a physical one.... For both the physicists and the moralists the preferred text was Homer, a choice dictated no doubt by the poet's place at the cultural center of the society and the consequent attention given to his works by literary exegetes at Alexandria and Pergamum."

14. From a strictly linguistic point of view, the *Koinè* dialect of the LXX, the NT, Josephus, and Philo descents mostly from the Attic which was the dialect of Aeschylus (525-456 BCE), Sophocles (496-406 BCE), Euripides (c. 480-406 BCE), and, of course, Plato (427-347 BCE) among other Athenian poets and philosophers. Attic in turn descents from Ionic, the dialect of Homer and Hesiod. For a discussion see Smyth, *Greek Grammar*, 3-4A. According to Smyth, "The Koinè took its rise in the Alexandrian period, so called from the preëminence of Alexandria in Egypt as a centre of learning until the Roman conquest of the East; and lasted to the end of the ancient world (sixth century A.D.)." The author and audience of 1 Timothy therefore share a linguistic heritage with Philo of Alexandria. However, with the sharing of a

then no need to show that the author and audience of 1 Timothy had direct knowledge of Plato or Philo as a way of accounting for the epistle's natalistic concept of virtue. The concept is simply *koinos topos* or a philosophical commonplace.[15]

Ephesus is also significant as the ancient center of the worship of Artemis (see Acts 19:24–41). Here is another promising avenue of investigation uncovered by the Clark Kroegers.[16] Although we cannot accept their central argument for the reinterpretation of 1 Tim 2:12, their characterization of 1 Tim 2:11–15 as a probable response to some features of the Artemis fertility cult is helpful. For the purposes of this study, the relevant feature of the Artemis cult would be language that associates the goddess with birthing or midwifery.[17] When Apuleius (c. 120–160 CE) identifies the Egyptian goddess Isis with Artemis (Diana) he says, "At another time you are Phoebus' sister; by applying to birth soothing remedies you relieve the pain of childbirth, and have brought teeming numbers to birth; now you are worshipped in the famed shrines of Ephesus" (*Metam.* 11.2).[18] At a much earlier time, Callimachus (310–235 BCE) spoke for Artemis and said, "I will dwell on the mountains and I will go to the cities of men only when women sorely distressed by the pangs of childbirth call upon me for help" (*Hymn. Dian.* 20–22). Plato, Callimachus, the author of Luke-Acts, Apuleius and the audiences for whom they wrote show that knowledge of Artemis lore and Ephesian culture was widespread and transgenerational even

---

linguistic heritage there must also be the inevitable sharing of other cultural legacies, such as a stock of familiar metaphors.

15. For a discussion of *koinos topos* ("common-place") in a different context see Kennedy, *Prog.*, 79–81.

16. Kroeger and Kroeger, *I Suffer Not A Woman*, 47–58, 105–13. See also McDonald, "Ephesus," 318–21.

17. Cf. Philo, *Migr.* 214 where the midwives of Exod 1:21 are "those souls which search for the invisible qualities" (αἱ ζητητικαὶ τῶν ἀφανῶν ψυχαί, *hai zētētikai tōn aphanōn psychai*) (cf. *Leg.* 3.3).

18. Welch, *Apuleius*, 219. Phoebus is another name for the sun-god Apollo. See the translation of Adlington and Gaselee, *The Golden Ass*, 541, where Artemis is addressed as the one "who hast saved so many people by lightening and lessening with thy medicines the pangs of travail" (*quae partu fetarum medelis lenientibus recreato populos tantos*).

beyond Ionia itself. One would expect that in cultures dominated by worship of a deity associated with childbirth, or at least in cultures knowledgeable about such worship, that the image of childbirth would be used in a variety of metaphorical senses.

In Plato's *Theaetetus*, for example, Socrates rehearses the legend of Artemis as the founder of the midwifery guild among mothers past the age of childbearing (*Theaet.* 149B–151E). Although Artemis was the patron goddess of childbirth, she herself was childless.[19] She honors the image of herself in post-reproductive mothers by assigning them the task of midwifing (μαιευτικός, *maieutikos*). Artemis does not choose women who have never been mothers because they lack experience. Socrates salutes midwives not only for their experience with pregnancy and motherhood, but also for their skills in pharmacology, incantation, and matchmaking. The works of midwives are therefore highly important.

Socrates then describes himself to Theaetetus as a midwife (μαῖα, *maia*) for the souls of men (he specifically means *men*, ἄνδρας, *andras*). His vocation is to help *men* "give birth to the manifold good things found within them." They cannot give birth by themselves. "But it is God and I, "Socrates says, "who delivers their children for them" (*Theaet.* 150D). Socrates criticizes those men who have failed to acknowledge his midwifing role after they had given birth. He also criticizes those who have left him for bad company and have "so greatly abused the children I helped them to birth that they lost them." According to Socrates, "they have caused miscarriage" (ἐξήμβλωσαν, *exēmblōsan*; root: ἀμβλίσκω, *ambliskō*) (*Theaet.* 150E). Those men who associate with Socrates are like women in childbirth, suffering the pains of labor. Their situation is indeed worse than that of parturient women because they suffer

19. Outside of Ephesus, Artemis was usually thought of as goddess of archery and hunting (Homer, *Il.* 16.184; Callimachus, *Hymn. Apoll.* 60). In this case, the role of goddess of childbirth was instead assigned to Eileithyia (Εἰλείθυια), daughter of Hera (Hesiod, *Theog.* 922; Homer, *Il.* 16.187; 19.103). Sometimes Homer uses a plural form of the reference, such as, "Eileithyiae, daughters of Hera" (Εἰλείθυιαι, Ἥρης θυγατέρες, *Eileithyiai, Hrēs Thygateres*) (*Il.* 11.270–71; 19.119). That Plato preserves the tradition of Artemis as goddess of childbirth along with that of Eileithyia in the same role (*Symp.* 206D) attests to the degree of Ionian-Ephesian influence in his thought.

day and night. Socrates suspects that Theaetetus is parturient, like a woman in labor (*Theaet.* 151A-C). The speech of Socrates in *Theaetetus* bears great interest and relevance, because it is here that he deploys the Artemis legend as a frame of reference for a metaphorical use of *childbearing*, and for explicating his own role in the birthing of *children*, with the *children* to be borne being specifically understood as *virtues*.[20]

It would be difficult to see how the author and audience of 1 Timothy could be oblivious to this frame of reference and similar metaphorical uses of childbearing in Ephesian culture, whether or not that audience actually resided in Ephesus. As acculturated *savants* of this Artemis mythology and language, and other birth-goddess lore, the author and audience of 1 Timothy would surely bring a metaphorical understanding to the use of "childbearing" in 1 Tim 2:15.

---

20. This same excavating for birthing metaphors occurs in Plato, *Symp.* 206D where we have the appearance of Eileithyia, patron goddess of childbirth. Diotima explains to Socrates that Eileithyia represents Beauty. The myth of the goddess is used as a frame of reference for speaking about the pregnant soul and her desire to give birth to beautiful things. Elsewhere, Pausanias (c. 174 CE) speaks about the cult of Eileithyia who had a sanctuary in Corinth among other places (Pausanias, *Descr.* 2. 35.11). The influence of such cults and their legends upon language, particularly in the metaphorical use of the image of childbearing, may be at least remotely reflected in early Christian use of natalistic language (Luke 7:35; Acts 17:28; John 3:3-7; 1 Cor 15.8; Gal 4:19, 26-27; 1 Thess 5:3; 1 Tim 2:15; Phlm 10; Jas 1:15, 18; 1 Pet 1:3; Rev 12:1-6).

4

Widening the View

Theology and History

SOTERIOLOGY AND VIRTUES-BEARING

More support for a new reading of 1 Tim 2:15 can be derived from a theological, or more specifically, soteriological description of 1 Timothy and the other Pastorals. We are not suggesting that there is a formal theology or soteriology contained within the Pastoral Epistles. What we actually have is a series of loosely connected affirmations. Yet these affirmations possess sufficient coherence and consistency to enable us to lay out a basic pattern of thought.[1] We are especially interested in the author's use of σωθῆναι, *sōthēnai*, "to save" (1 Tim 2:4) and cognate terms. Salvation is ultimately an eschatological and apocalyptic event.[2] It is the central event in a scenario precipitated by the coming of Christ at the end of the age (1 Tim 6:14–15; 2 Tim 4:1; Titus 2:13). Eschatological salvation is corporate in scope (2 Tim 4:8; Titus 3:7), but personally apprehended (2 Tim 2:10–13; 4:8, 18). For the collective of believers it means "eternal life" (1 Tim 6:19; Titus 1:2; 3:7), "eternal glory"

---

1. See Young, *The Theology of the Pastoral Letters*, 2–3.
2. Young, *The Theology of the Pastoral Letters*, 57–59.

(2 Tim 2:10), "the crown of righteousness" (2 Tim 4:8), and life in God's "heavenly kingdom" (2 Tim 4:18). Eschatological salvation is preceded by the judgment of the living and the dead, and awarded to those who are found "rich in good works" (1 Tim 6:18) and have lived according to "sound doctrine" (1 Tim 4:16; 2 Tim 4:1).[3]

There is, however, a second sense of salvation in the Pastoral Epistles. It is a realized sense.[4] The believer takes possession of future salvation in the present (1 Tim 6:12; 2 Tim 1:10; Titus 2:11; 3:5).[5] Salvation is realized when people "lay hold on to sound doctrine" (2 Tim 1:13), "come to a knowledge of the truth" (1 Tim 2:4; 2 Tim 2:25), and "cleanse themselves" of vice (2 Tim 2:21). Saving knowledge, which elicits faith, is communicated through the gospel of Jesus Christ (2 Tim 1:10)—a ministry of preaching and teaching that includes exposition of "the holy writings" (2 Tim 3:15-16). In this case, saving knowledge seems equivalent to "faith in Jesus Christ" (2 Tim 3:15). One receives salvation in the here and now when one accepts this knowledge.[6]

Realized salvation is nevertheless not according to works, here understood as virtuous works, but according to grace (2 Tim 1:9; Titus 2:11; 3:5).[7] Grace is both God's merciful disposition toward us (1 Tim 1:2, 13-14) and God's powerful presence with us (2 Tim 2:2; 4:17, 22; Titus 3:15).[8] As mercy, God's grace was expressed through the self-sacrifice of Jesus whose death effected liberation or ransom from sin (1 Tim 2:6; Titus 2:14). As presence, God's grace is experienced as the Holy Spirit, which gives life (1 Tim 6:13; 2 Tim 1:7, 14).[9] Grace was first mediated to us through Jesus Christ prior to

---

3. See Donelson, *Colossians, Ephesians, 1 and 2 Timothy and Titus*, 146-50.

4. See Towner, "The Portrait of Paul," 169.

5. From a broad perspective, any distinction between realized and eschatological salvation is quite artificial. In the believer's experience, the possession of one is the possession of the other, as the author of the Pastoral Epistles indicates (1 Tim 6:12; Titus 2:11; 3:7). However, the distinction becomes necessary in order to more clearly show how salvation is related to virtues-bearing.

6. See Young, *The Theology of the Pastoral Letters*, 58-59.

7. See Johnson, *The First and Second Letters to Timothy*, 348.

8. Johnson, *The First and Second Letters to Timothy*, 347-48, 355.

9. See Young, *The Theology of the Pastoral Letters*, 68-70.

Women, Salvation, and Childbearing

creation and then during his earthly sojourn (2 Tim 1:9-10; 2:5). Grace continues to be mediated to us through his spiritual presence as resurrected Lord (1 Tim 1:14; 2 Tim 2:11). In either case, when God's grace through Jesus Christ is acknowledged and accepted it elicits the response of faith.

Various senses of faith occur in the Pastoral Epistles. At times, faith means assent to sound doctrine (1 Tim 1:4; 3:9; 2 Tim 1:13; 2:2). At times, faith appears as the content of sound doctrine (1 Tim 4:6; 2 Tim 3:15; 4:7; Titus 1:4, 13; 2:2). At other times, faith is a virtue of the soul among other virtues (1 Tim 2:15; 4:12; 6:11; 2 Tim 1:5; 2:22).[10] However, as a response to grace, faith is an act of bonding with God or Christ through self-surrender in a committed relationship (2 Tim 1:12; 2:19; 3:17). This faith as *bonding* is manifested outwardly in the life of the believer through acts that mirror the character of God or Christ (1 Tim 1:16; 2 Tim 1:13; Titus 2:11-14).[11] Although these acts would be called virtues elsewhere, in the Pastoral Epistles they are called acts of righteousness, godliness, faith, love, endurance, gentleness, or simply good works (1 Tim 5:25; 6:11, 18; 2 Tim 2:21; 3:17).[12]

In the Pauline corpus as a whole, virtues are understood variously as inwardly possessed gifts of God or the Holy Spirit (Rom 15:13; Gal 5:22-25; 1 Tim 1:2, 14, 19; 2 Tim 1:2, 5-7), willfully cultivated aspects of the human spirit (Rom 12:9-21; 1 Cor 13:4-7, 13; 2 Tim 2:22), or outward expressions of a righteous character (Rom 12:13; 1 Cor 16:14; Gal 6:10; 2 Thess 1:4; 1 Tim 2:15; 3:2-4, 8-13; 5:25; Eph 4:25-32).[13] In all three cases, virtues are consequent to realized salvation (Rom 13:11-14; Eph 4:21-24; 1 Cor 2:14; 15:58; Titus 2:11-14; 3:8), but antecedent to eschatological salvation (Gal 6:8; 2 Thess 1:5; 2:13-17; 1 Tim 4:8-10; 6:11-12, 18-19; Titus 3:3-7).[14] First Timothy 2:15 seems to share more in this third

---

10. See Johnson, *The First and Second Letters to Timothy*, 153; Marshall and Towner, *The Pastoral Epistles*, 120.

11. See Johnson, *The First and Second Letters to Timothy*, 179, 183.

12. See Donelson, *Colossians, Ephesians, 1 and 2 Timothy, and Titus*, 131-33.

13. See Johnson, *The First and Second Letters to Timothy*, 182-83; Young, *The Theology of the Pastoral Letters*, 37-39.

14. See Young, *The Theology of the Pastoral Letters*, 28-31, 57-59.

sense of virtues as outward expressions of a righteous character. This is not to suggest, however, that 1 Tim 2:15 is entirely free of ambiguity in its evocation of virtue ethics. In context, the four virtues of 1 Tim 2:15 are both inward dispositions (1 Tim 4:14; 2 Tim 1:5-6) and outward expressions (1 Tim 2:2; 3:2-4; 5:9-10, 25; 6:11; 2 Tim 2:22; 3:10; 4:5; Titus 1:7-9; 2:3-8), and both signs of realized salvation (1 Tim 1:5) and means of eschatological salvation (1 Tim 1:16; 4:15-16; 2 Tim 4:7-8). However, in 1 Tim 2:15 the emphasis appears to be upon the outward expression of virtues as the means of eschatological salvation (cf. Rom 2:6-7; 2 Cor 5:10). The performance of these works somehow builds up merit or "store up treasure" that will guarantee one's salvation in the eschatological future (1 Tim 6:18-19).[15]

Both God and Christ are Savior (1 Tim 1:1; 2:3; 2 Tim 1:10; Titus 1:3, 4; 2:10; 3:4, 6).[16] It almost seems that God is primarily Savior in an eschatological context and Christ is primarily Savior in a realized context, but we cannot be altogether certain that this is what the author is thinking. At one point it is not clear whether God is again being called Savior or Christ is being called God (Titus 2:13; cf. Rom 9:5).[17] It is at least clear that the roles of God and Christ as Savior converge insofar as God has acted in and through Christ to bring salvation to all (1 Tim 2:3-6; 2 Tim 1:8-10; Titus 2:11-14; 3:4-8).[18]

We come to a critical point with the observation that "God our Savior wants all people (πάντας ἀνθρώπους, *pantas anthrōpous*) to be saved and to come to a knowledge of the truth" (1 Tim 2:3-4). This inclusive aspect of the author's message is a recurring theme. The author wishes that petitions, prayers, intercessions, and thanksgivings be made for "all people" (πάντων ἀνθρώπων,

---

15. See Marshall and Towner, *The Pastoral Epistles*, 673.

16. This may or may not be a self-conscious rejection of the idea of the Roman Emperor as Savior. Kelly feels that the author is simply speaking in accordance with Jewish theology and tradition when he applies the title Savior to God as well as to Christ (*A Commentary on the Pastoral Epistles*, 40).

17. See Collins, "The Theology of the Epistle to Titus," 71-72; Thurston, "The Theology of Titus," 179.

18. See Couser, "God and Christian Existence," 283.

Women, Salvation, and Childbearing

pantōn anthrōpōn) (1 Tim 2:1). Christ gave himself as a ransom for "all" (πάντων, *pantōn*)(1 Tim 2:6). God is the savior of "all people," (πάντων ἀνθρώπων, *pantōn anthrōpōn*) especially those who believe (1 Tim 4:10). The author exhorts "everyone [πᾶς, *pas*] who names the name of the Lord to depart from unrighteousness" (2 Tim 2:19). "The grace of God has appeared bringing salvation to all people" (πᾶσιν ἀνθρώποις, *pasin anthrōpois*) (Titus 2:11).

It is probable that these "all" terms used by the author are gender as well as ethnically-inclusive, and perhaps even primarily gender-inclusive. Although there is mention of Gentiles in the Pastoral Epistles (1 Tim 2:7; 3:16; 2 Tim 1:11; 4:17), we do not find an explicit Jew-Gentile dichotomy (cf. Rom 1:16; 2:10; 3:30). Instead we find an explicit male-female dichotomy. Furthermore, when the author wishes to be gender-specific he uses restrictive terms (ἄνδρα, ἄνδρας, γυνή, γυναίκας, *andra, andras, gynē, gynaikas,* man, men, woman, women, 1 Tim 2:8–12; 3:2, 11–12).[19] His use of inclusive terms in a soteriological context therefore appears to be more than casual.

We come to an equally critical point with the observation that the means of salvation are the same for *all*, without regard to gender. These closely-related references to saving knowledge (1 Tim 2:4), the ransoming death of Christ (1 Tim 2:6), saving faith (1 Tim 4:10), and the grace of God (Titus 2:11) are inseparable from the inclusive statements already mentioned. If both genders are included in these "all" phrases, then the author of the Pastoral Epistles believes that the means of salvation for women and men are the same (cf. Gal 3:28). We must then ask how to reconcile this observation with the seemingly gender-specific idea of salvation through childbearing.[20] At this point, the solution seems readily available in the literary-cultural background of the idea.

---

19. See Marshall and Towner, *The Pastoral Epistles*, 425–28. As they show in their survey of interpretive options for 1 Tim 2:4, not much attention has been given to the possibility of gender-inclusiveness in the epistle's use of "all."

20. See the survey of attempts to address this question in Marshall and Towner, *The Pastoral Epistles*, 467–70. They observe, "Its meaning is a puzzle, and a number of interpretations have been offered."

Why then should we suppose that the author and audience of 1 Timothy have an understanding of childbearing that is similar to metaphorical uses in Hellenistic virtue ethics? Why then should we abandon a literal "plain sense" reading of 1 Tim 2:15? The answer is threefold. First, the form of the statement, with "childbearing" in the apodosis and four virtues listed in the protasis, is similar to other literary expressions in that culture where children become metaphors for virtues (e.g., Plato, *Symp.* 209D–E; Philo, *Gig.* 5; *Deus* 117–18). Second, such a supposition places a theologically and historically coherent reading of 1 Timothy over against an incoherent one. Third, this dual coherence in itself exists at four levels: within the epistle of 1 Timothy, within the corpus of the Pastoral Epistles, within the Pauline corpus as a whole, and, at least historically speaking, within the Hellenistic environment of the NT. The availability of both extrabiblical and intertexual literary evidence for a coherent reading of a notoriously difficult biblical text cannot be merely fortuitous, especially when the two kinds of evidence are culturally contemporaneous. Unless we want to assign all such correspondences in historical studies to happenstance, our metaphorical understanding of childbearing in 1 Tim 2:15 is more probable than the glaring contradiction posed by a literal, "plain sense" reading. It is true that metaphorical and literal interpretations are not always mutually exclusive. Even though Philo, for example, interprets the child of Sarah as virtue, he does believe that there was actually a flesh and blood Isaac. However, there can be no literal understanding of childbearing as a means of salvation in 1 Tim 2:15, precisely because childbearing is here linked to salvation as its means. A theological and historical investigation precludes such literalism.

It should also be acknowledged that the understanding of salvation in 1 Timothy and the other Pastorals is not altogether congruent with how salvation is understood in Plato or Philo. In Hellenistic virtue ethics, salvation is mostly the attainment of sound-mindedness, self-control, and self-sufficiency (Plato, *Resp.* 3.389 D; Philo, *Virt.* 14–16). This is not the salvation that furthermore means forgiveness of sins, escape from divine wrath, fellowship with God, and life eternal, such as we find in the Pastorals. Our point is not that the author of 1 Timothy shares a common understanding of salvation with Plato and Philo, but that they draw upon a common metaphorical use of "childbearing."

1 TIMOTHY 2:15 IN THE HISTORY OF BIBLICAL INTERPRETATION

In the history of biblical interpretation, a literal understanding of childbearing in 1 Tim 2:15 is assumed by Clement of Alexandria (150–215 CE), Gregory of Nyssa (330–395 CE), Theodore of Mopsuestia (350–428 CE), Ambrosiaster (c. 370 CE), and Pelagius (c. 415 CE).[21] However, in *Strom.* 3.12.90, Clement altogether ignores the subject of 1 Tim 2:15. It is the man who is the husband of one wife who finds salvation by bringing children into the world. For Gregory, the text refers to the salvation of the mother who bears spiritually regenerated children. Theodore only stipulates further that all women, not just Eve, will be saved through childbearing. Ambroiaster adds the qualification that the salvation which comes through childbearing only applies to women whose children are "reborn in Christ." Pelagius explains that when Paul speaks of the salvation that comes through childbearing, he is referring only to the baptism and spiritual rebirth to which children are brought by their believing mother.

The period between Pelagius and the Reformation is a wide gap, but one finds nothing new or notable in this gap regarding the exegesis of our text. Martin Luther (1483–1546) will still offer us little to celebrate in his appropriations of 1 Tim 2:15. He understood that salvation through literal childbirth applies only to the married woman who lives by the Word of God and faith.[22] In another place,

---

21. See Gorday, *Colossians, 1–2 Thessalonians, 1–2 Timothy, Titus, Philemon*, 167 for citations of Theodore, Ambrosiaster, Pelagius, and Gregory on 1 Tim 2:15. Origen of Alexandria (185–254 CE) is also cited, but Origen is actually commenting on *The Song of Songs* when he speaks allegorically of a "chaste begetting of children" as a result of marital union between Christ and the church or between Christ and the "blessed soul" as an individual member of the church. It is not clear whether the "children" themselves are anything other than members of the church.

22. Luther, *Lectures*, 5.

however, the verse means that God will not reject infants "because of pimples, filth, and troubles provided they persevere in faith and love." God "has patience in many infirmities."[23]

John Calvin (1509-64) also understood "childbearing" in 1 Tim 2:15 in the literal sense. He maintained, however, that women are saved through childbearing as an act of obedience. But more than childbearing is being referred to here. The Apostle is also speaking of the pains and distresses associated with childbirth and the rearing of children. Nevertheless, obedience in these matters is acceptable to God only if it proceeds from faith, love, sanctification, and sobriety.[24] Again, there is nothing new or notable in the exegesis of our text in the period between Calvin and twentieth century biblical scholarship.

It is only when we backtrack to Augustine of Hippo (354-430 CE) that we find an interpretation of 1 Tim 2:15 that especially peaks our interest. In *Trin.* 12.7.11, Augustine maintains that Paul's teaching—that the woman is "brought to salvation by childbearing" (*saluam fieri per filiorum generationem*)—is to be understood "figuratively and mystically" (*figurate ac mystice*). Augustine, however, is here chiefly addressing the conundrum of why a woman is required in 1 Cor 11:5-7 to wear a veil over her head if she is also made in the image of God, as we are told in Gen 1:27. Augustine explains that it is both the man and woman together who are the image of God. Yet, when standing alone, the man remains the image of God, while the woman, when standing alone, does not. This is because the man in the Genesis text represents the human mind directed toward spiritual things, while the woman represents the human mind directed toward temporal things. When the human mind is both directed toward the spiritual and distracted by the temporal it is still the image of God. However, it is only the spiritually directed side of the mind that is the image of God when standing alone, while the temporally directed side when standing alone is not. It is obvious that Augustine is straining at this point. In any case, the veil on the woman's head represents the restraining influence of the

---

23. Luther, *Lectures*, 312.
24. Calvin, *Commentaries*, 71-72.

spiritually focused side of the mind upon the temporally focused side of the mind.

To prove that Paul's teaching in 1 Cor 11:5-7 and other places should be interpreted in this figurative and mystical way, Augustine cites 1 Tim 5:5 where the widow who is bereft of children and nephews has nevertheless placed her trust in God and prays constantly. For Augustine (and this is quite a leap) the widow of 1 Tim 5:5 illustrates the deceived woman and transgressor who is brought to salvation by childbearing, but only if "they" continue in "faith, and charity, and holiness, with sobriety."[25] Augustine understands "they" as a reference to the widow's children. However, Augustine finds it untenable that a widow could be deprived of salvation if she had no children, or if the children she had did not continue in good works. Therefore, like the veil on the woman's head, "children" must be understood figuratively and mystically. According to Augustine, "good works are, as it were, the children of our lives" (*opera bona tamquam filii sunt vitae nostrae*). Although Augustine sees "good works as children" in the apodosis of 1 Tim 2:15, he disappointingly does not explicitly identify good works with the four virtues listed in the protasis. Furthermore, it is not historical and literary evidence, but wild logic and a dogmatic allegorizing hermeneutic that forms the basis for his conclusions. Since my interpretation of 1 Tim 2:15 is based upon historical, cultural, and literary evidence it is not quite correct to describe my approach as "Augustinian" as a few people have done. Nevertheless, in the history of biblical interpretation, it is Augustine who comes closest to the understanding of 1 Tim 2:15 advocated in this book. Later, in *Civ.* 10.3, Augustine will say that it is by God's embrace that "the intellectual soul is impregnated and made to give birth to true virtues" (*anima intellectualis incorporeo . . . veris impletur fecundaturque virtutibus*). Augustine in no way directly relates this observation to 1 Tim 2:15, but it certainly reflects the Platonic-Philonic perspective that characterizes both the time of Augustine and the time of 1 Timothy several centuries earlier. Therefore, our brief encounter with Augustine is the only glimmer of direct Christian precedence for my interpretation of 1 Tim 2:15.

25. Schaff, *Augustin*, 159.

Perhaps, he would have offered us more had he engaged the text of 1 Tim 2:15 more directly.

THE CONVERGENCE OF EVIDENCE

It might finally be asked, to which stream of influence do we assign the greatest weight in our argument for an allegorical and natalistic interpretation of 1 Tim 2:15? Is it Greek mythology, Ionian philosophy, Platonic or Philonic thought, Hellenistic virtue ethics, Jewish and early Christian background, Gnostic background, Ephesian culture and Artemis lore, or an apparently synonymous agricultural metaphor and generative concept in the undisputed and disputed Pauline Epistles? Answering this question would seem like an unnecessary exercise. If it were not the case that all of these influences weigh heavily upon our argument, it would surely be a few of them. But given the demonstrable historical and literary interrelationship of these streams of influence, how could we isolate a few from all the rest? How could we isolate only one from the rest? It seems that we should simply acknowledge the weighty relevance of all of these streams of influence in this argument.

Therefore, in regard to the hermeneutics of 1 Tim 2:15 in particular, our investigation leaves us with two possibilities. Either the author and audience of 1 Timothy understand the four virtues of 1 Tim 2:15 as *children*, that is to say, as the products of "childbearing," or we have a soteriological idea in 1 Tim 2:15 (i.e., the idea that women are saved through literal childbirth) that is both unprecedented and uncorroborated in the whole of the Pauline corpus *and its literary-cultural environment*. In light of the religio–philosophical evidence herein discussed, we must ask, Which is most likely, the former or the latter case?

VIRTUES AS CHILDREN IN PAULINE CONTEXT

"Childbearing" in 1 Tim 2:15 is therefore a metaphor for "virtues-bearing." It is the final metaphor in a thoroughly allegorical parenesis. One advantage of this new reading of 1 Tim 2:11–15 over

Women, Salvation, and Childbearing

traditional ones is that it more clearly shows how "saved through childbearing" coheres with the typical Pauline notion of "saved by faith" (Rom 1:16; 10:9-10; 2 Tim 3:15; Eph 2:8).[26] Our reading also more clearly shows how "saved through childbearing" coheres with the typical Pauline notions of "love as the fulfillment of the law" (Rom 13:10), "fruit unto holiness" (Rom 6:22; cf. Heb 12:14), and "working out your soul salvation with fear and trembling" (Phil 2:12). Therefore, we have reason to retire patently non-Pauline notions like the salvation of women based upon their ability to bear children in the literal sense. For the author of 1 Timothy, the means of salvation for women, remains the same as the means of salvation for men, and vice-versa.[27] *All women and men must give birth to and continue in faith, love, holiness, and temperance in order to be saved.* The author of 1 Timothy implies as much in 4:12. "Let no one despise your youth, but be an example to the believers in word, in conduct [ἀναστροφῇ, *anastrophē*], in love, in faith, and in purity [ἁγνεία, *hagneia*]" (cf. Titus 2:11-12). Despite questions over the authorship of 1 Timothy, there is no question that the author of 1 Timothy belongs to the "Pauline school."[28] In no other way does the author of 1 Timothy present an idea that is incompatible with the thought of the undisputed Pauline letters (cf. Rom 7:7-12; 1 Tim 1:8-11). It is therefore highly unlikely that the author of this epistle would depart so greatly from typical Pauline thought that he would suggest that literal childbirth is somehow important for the salvation of women.

---

26. Cf. "saved by hope" (Rom 8:24) and "saved by grace" (Eph 2:5; 2 Tim 1:9). Cf. also "justified by faith" (Rom 3:28; Gal 2:16) and "justified by grace" (Titus 3:7).

27. See Kroeger and Kroeger, *I Suffer Not A Woman*, 171, 177; Coupland, "Salvation through Childbearing," 303. This is ultimately the point that the Kroegers and Coupland want to make. But their literal understanding of the reference to "childbearing" forces them to make this point in spite of rather than because of the reference.

28. See Meeks, *The First Urban Christians*, 82-84; Standhartinger, "Colossians and the Pauline School," 572-93.

5

Tying in the Theme
Women in the Letters of Paul

CONSISTENCY AND COHERENCE

There is a school of thought within Pauline Studies that summarily assigns inconsistency and incoherence to Pauline thought whether the focus is upon the undisputed or disputed letters.[1] My study is a counterpoint to this line of thinking. I align myself with those scholars who have discovered the consistency and coherence of Pauline thought through a deep reading of the letters where the author's rhetorical techniques and strategies are most clearly revealed.[2]

For the purpose of this chapter, which is to demonstrate the consistency and coherence of the Pauline Letters regarding women, I will for the time being set aside the debate over the authorship of these letters. I will simply speak of Paul as the author of all the letters that bear his name. With that said, I call attention to Paul's acknowledgement that the sincere faith of Timothy appeared first in

---

1. See Räisänen, *Paul and the Law*, 264; Sanders, *Paul and Palestinian Judaism*, 550–52.

2. See Johnson, "Romans 9–11," 220, 232–33; Hays, *Echoes of Scripture*, xii, 13–14, 20–23; Lodge, *Romans 9–11*, x–xiii, 21–35; Dunn, "Paul's Epistle to the Romans," 2843–74.

his grandmother Lois and his mother Eunice, and was now in him (2 Tim 1:5).[3] Paul therefore gives us a brief genealogy of Timothy's faith. We first ask if Paul is speaking of "saving faith" in the case of Lois, Eunice, and Timothy. A positive answer to this question is implied throughout the Pastoral Epistles; nevertheless, we also have more explicit references to saving faith in this literature (1 Tim 1:16; 4:10, 16; 6:12; 2 Tim 3:15).

We next ask if this "saving faith" has anything to do with childbearing literally understood. We ask this only because there are those who will still insist upon reading *teknogonia* in 1 Tim 2:15 as a reference to childbearing literally understood. Even if we thought that literal childbearing had anything to do with Lois and Eunice's salvation, we would naturally have to rule that out in the case of Timothy. Yet it is obvious that Paul is speaking of the same kind of faith in Lois, Eunice, and Timothy. The genealogical sequence requires an equivalency of faith at least in terms of kind. This would mean that this faith and the salvation it brings has nothing to do with childbearing literally understood. We are back to affirming that only childbearing understood as a metaphor for "virtues-bearing" makes sense. If we must apply 1 Tim 2:15 to the saving faith of Lois, Eunice, and Timothy then this virtue for each of them is a "child" of their soul, along with the other children—love, holiness, and temperance.

An altogether different, but still relevant observation also emerges simply from the prominent mention of Lois and Eunice in 2 Tim 1:5. The mention of these two women in this context is consistent with the prominent mention of women throughout the Pauline Letters, and bears implications for how Paul views women generally speaking and in the Christian mission. We therefore come to a discussion of 1 Tim 2:11–15 within the larger scope of Paul's view of women. The egalitarian view of women that we discern in 1 Tim 2:11–15 should be consistent with the view of women that we

---

3. Dunn ("The First and Second Letters," 833), includes Acts 16:1 in his reflections on 2 Tim 1:5. He presented two alternatives: that the reference may be to Timothy's faith as a third generation Christian, or to his Christian faith in "direct continuity with the typical piety of a Jewish home."

discern in the rest of the Pauline writings.[4] Our intention is to show that the two views are indeed consistent.

Even before we leave the Pastoral Epistles, we are struck by Paul's mention of "Prisca and Aquila" in 2 Tim 4:19: "Greet Prisca and Aquila, and the household of Onesiphoros." Prisca is female. Aquila is male. They are married. We meet this wife and husband ministry team in the NT canon first in Acts 18:1–4, 18–22, 24–26; and then we meet them again in Rom 16:3, 1 Cor 16:19, and 2 Tim 4:19. The name Prisca in 2 Tim, and in the Roman and Corinthian correspondence, is a variation of the name Priscilla, which is written in Acts. The striking feature of the couple's mention in Acts 18:18, 26; Rom 16:3; and 2 Tim 4:19, is that, in these places, Prisca is mentioned first. This is probably because of Prisca's prominence and leadership as the pastor of a house church in Rome (Acts 18:2; Rom 16:5), or Ephesus (1 Cor 16:19; 2 Tim 4:19), or in both places at different times. Chloe also seems to serve this pastoral role in Corinth (1 Cor 1:11). Nympha also serves as the head of a house church in Colossae or Laodicea (Col 4:15). Apphia, who shares leadership of a house church in Colossae, is also mentioned (Phlm 2).

When Paul mentions women in their roles as servants and leaders in the Christian mission, Paul uses the same terms that he uses for men. Phoebe is identified as a "minister" (διάκονος, *diakonos*) of the church in Cenchreae, and a "patron" (προστάτις, *prostatis*) of many people including Paul (Rom 16:1–2). Paul also applies this title "minister" to himself (1 Cor 3:5; 2 Cor 3:6; Col 1:23, 25), Epaphras (Col 1:7), Tychicus (Col 4:7), and to other male leaders of the church (Phil 1:1; 1 Tim 3:8, 12).[5]

---

4. The term "egalitarian," as I use it, describes a view of women and men as fully equal in role, status, potential, opportunity, and authority in any and all settings, but particularly in the ministry and mission of the church. My use of the term is not to be identified with egalitarian ideologies that erase gender identities or reduce gender to a mere social construct. See Skalko, "The Incoherence of Gender," 1–2.

5. While commenting on Titus 1:5–9 and the equivalent terms "bishop" and "elder," Andria ("1 Timothy, 2 Timothy, Titus," 1483) says that Paul's words cannot be appealed to in arguments over whether women can be elders, "However," he says, "1 Timothy 3:11 does suggest that women may serve as deacons."

Women, Salvation, and Childbearing

Paul refers only to Phoebe as a patron. In Greco-Roman culture, the title "patron" carries prestige and implies that the individual is a person of wealth and influence (Cicero, *Pis.* 25; Appian, *Bell. civ.* 2.14; Cassius Dio, *Rom. hist.* 74). In Luke 8:3 the women who followed Jesus fulfill this role.

There is also an equivalency in function and mission that appears in the mention of Phoebe. She appears to be the carrier of the Letter to the Romans. This trusted and critical role as a Pauline Letter carrier is also fulfilled seemingly by Tychicus (Eph 6:31; Col 4:7; Titus 3:12), Onesimus (Col 4:8; Phlm 12), Artemas (Titus 3:12), Timothy (1 Cor 16:10; 1 Thess 3:2), Titus (2 Cor 7:6, 13), and Epaphras (Col 1:7).

Paul also describes Prisca and Aquila as "my co-workers in Christ Jesus, who risked their own necks for my life, for whom not only I am thankful but all the churches of the Gentiles" (τοὺς συνεργούς μου ἐν Χριστῷ Ἰησοῦ οἵτινες ὑπὲρ τῆς ψυχῆς μου τὸν ἑαυτῶν τράχηλων ὑπέθηκαν οἷς οὐκ ἐγὼ μόνος εὐχαριστῶ ἀλλὰ καὶ πᾶσαι αἱ ἐκκλησίαι τῶν ἐθνῶν, *tous synergous mou en Christō Iēsou hoitines hyper tēs psychēs mou ton eautōn trachēlōn hypethēkan hois ouk egō monos eucharistō alla kai pasai hai ekklēsiai tōn ethnōn*) (Rom 16:3). Paul also speaks of the women Euodia and Syntyche with "the rest of my co-workers" (τῶν λοιπῶν συνεργῶν μου, *tōn loipōn synergōn mou*)(Phil 4:2). Paul also uses this term co-worker (συνεργός, *synergos*) to describe Apollos (1 Cor 3:9), Titus (2 Cor 8:23), Timothy (Rom 16:21; 1 Thess 3:2), Urbanus (Rom 16:9), and, of course, Clement (Phil 4:3). When Paul speaks of how Prisca and Aquila risked their lives for his, he makes no distinction between the two in the level of dangers they faced, nor does he show any difference in the level of gratitude shown toward them by the church. Paul makes no distinction between Prisca and any male in this regard. When it comes to facing danger on behalf of the Christian mission, Prisca is equal to Paul himself (2 Cor 6:4–5; 11:23–33; 2 Tim 4:15–18) and other male missionaries who faced danger. Epaphroditus is a male missionary who nearly died of illness while on the mission field (Phil 2:25–30). Paul urges the Philippians to honor Epaphroditus for "risking his life" (παραβολευσάμενος τῇ ψυχῇ, *paraboleusamenos tē psychē*) for Paul and the work of Christ

TYING IN THE THEME

(Phil 2:30). Notably, Prisca is no less honored as a co-worker who risked her life for Paul and the Christian mission.

THE EVIDENCE FOR THE APOSTLE JUNIA

The most celebrated indicator of Paul's attitude toward women in the mission field may very well occur in Rom 16:7 where Paul says, "Greet Andronicus and Junia my kinspeople and fellow prisoners, who are prominent among the apostles, and who were before me in Christ" (σπάσασθε Ἀνδρόνικον καὶ Ἰουνίον τοὺς συγγενεῖς μου καὶ συναιχμαλώτους μου, οἵτινές εἰσιν ἐπίσημοι ἐν τοῖς ἀποστόλοις, οἳ καὶ πρὸ ἐμοῦ γέγοναν ἐν Χριστῷ, *aspasasthe Andronikon kai Iounion tous syngeneis mou kai synaichmalōtous mou, oitines eisin episēmoi en tois apostolois hoi kai pro emou gegonan en Christō*). Andronicus is male. Junia is female. We are not sure about how to describe their relationship. Much depends upon what Paul means when he refers to them both as his kinspeople. Most significantly, they are both referred to as apostles.

An apostle is the highest level of leadership and authority in the Christian mission (1 Cor 12:28-29; Eph 4:11). It is even a higher office than bishop or elder. In 2 Cor 8:23 and Phil 2:25 Paul uses the term in a lesser sense as "messenger," but when he uses the term to refer to the collective leadership of the Christian mission (*the* apostles) his meaning is very specific. The chief criterion for being an apostle is to be an eye-witness to the resurrection of Jesus Christ (Acts 1:22; 1 Cor 9:1; 15:5-11; Gal 1:16). Moreover, this experience must occur during the eyewitness period of Christian history, that is to say, during that period when a number of the first eyewitnesses to the resurrection of Jesus were still alive (Acts 1:21-22; John 21:20-24; 1 Cor 15:6; 2 Pet 1:16-19; 1 John 1:1-4). For this reason, there can be no more apostles in this specific sense after the death of the last living original eyewitness to the resurrection of Jesus Christ.[6] An apostle must also be *sent* (ἀποστέλλω, *apostellō*) by Jesus, the very act from which the term apostle is derived (Matt 10:16; Luke 10:3; John 13:20; 17:18; 20:21; 1 Cor 1:17).

---

6. Waters, "Empire and the Johannine Epistles," 556-57.

Andronicus and Junia are also honorably referred to as "fellow-prisoners" (συναιχμαλώτους, *synaichmalōtous*) of Paul. There is no distinction made between the two in this regard. Notably, the males Epaphras and Aristarchus are also honorably and separately referred to as a fellow-prisoner (συναιχμάλωτός, *synaichmalōtos*) of Paul (Col 4:10; Phlm 23). Junia is no less honorably mentioned as a fellow-prisoner.

The designation of Junia as an apostle has not gone unquestioned. Some attention should be given to the debate. Al Wolters acknowledges a "broad consensus" in the scholarly community that IOYNIAN (*IOUNIAN*) in Rom 16:7 should be interpreted as a female name (Ἰουνίαν, *Iounian*, Junia).[7] This is a consensus convened by scholars like Bernadette Brooten and Eldon Jay Epp.[8] Bruce Metzger pointed out that some manuscripts, such as Papyrus 46 (third century), the Bohairic Coptic version (third century), and Ambrosiaster (fourth century) replace IOYNIAN (*IOUNIAN*) with IOYΛIAN (*IOULIAN*, Julia) through scribal error (the assimilation of a name read in Rom 16:15). However, IOUNIAN is the best attested reading.[9]

In the accented Greek texts written with small letters (minuscules), Ἰουνιᾶν (with a circumflex) indicates a male name, and Ἰουνίαν (with an acute accent) indicates a female name. Most early Christian interpreters of Romans favor the feminine rendering of the name. *Junia* is the name in its Latin form.

Wolters, however, challenges the consensus. He suggests that the name *IOUNIAN* may be the Greek transliteration of a masculine Semitic, specifically Hebrew name. He argues for *Yĕḥunnī* (יוחי) as that name. This name is probably a shortened form of (וּ)הְיֻנֵּי (*Yĕḥunnīyāḥ* [*û*]), "may Yahweh be gracious."[10]

In the LXX, as Wolter explains, there are a number of Greek names that begin with Ἰου– and that represents Hebrew names in which the second letter is a guttural (for example, Ἰούδας, *Ioudas*

---

7. Wolters, "IOYNIAN," 397.
8. Brooten, "Junia," 141–44; Epp, *Junia*.
9. Metzger, *A Textual Commentary*, 539.
10. Wolters, "IOYNIAN," 398, 400.

Tying in the Theme

represents *Yĕhûdâ*). Also, there are many Hebrew names that have been turned into Greek masculine names (like Νικίας or Λυσίας, *Nikias* or *Lysias*) which have the -ίου genitive (possessive) ending or the -ίαν accusative (direct object) ending. These are called first declension masculine nouns.[11] Wolters says:

> By analogy with these names, IOYNIAN could well be the accusative of a masculine name, as illustrated by Matt 1:8–11, where four such masculine names occur in the accusative in quick succession: Ὀζίαν, Ἐζεκίαν, Ἰωσίαν, and Ἰεχονίαν.[12]

Wolters therefore rejects the premise that Ἰουνίαν (with an acute accent) was understood as a feminine name by ancient scribes. Wolters follows H. St. J. Thackeray in noting that many Hebrew masculine names end in an abbreviation of the divine name Yahweh (־הִי, *yah*). In the LXX, these names usually end in -ίας.[13] Wolters argues then that IOYNIAN may be reasonably taken as the masculine name Ἰουνίας (Junias), which is in turn the Greek form of the Hebrew name *Yĕḥunnī*.[14] Wolters further supports his argument with reference to phonological rules governing Hebrew name formation and epigraphic evidence for the name *Yĕḥunnī*.[15]

Wolters acknowledges that the name Ἰουνίας, *Iounias* (Junias) does not occur elsewhere, but he observes that the Hebrew original *Yĕḥunnī* occurs rarely, and outside of the Hebrew Bible. Therefore, it comes as no surprise that we do not see the name Junias outside of Rom 16:7. Some scholars see this is a major weakness in Wolter's argument. First, it is only speculation that this Hebrew name lies behind the Greek name, and then the Greek name itself is unattested in the Greco-Roman world at the time of Paul.

Wolter accepts that the question remains whether IOYNIAN, *IOUNIAN* in Rom 16:7 derives from a Hebrew masculine name

---

11. Wolters, "IOYNIAN," 398–99.
12. Wolters, "IOYNIAN," 399. The names transliterate as Ozian, Hezekian, Iōsian, and Iechonian (Uzziah, Hezekiah, Josiah, and Jechoniah).
13. Wolters, "IOYNIAN," 399.
14. Wolters, "IOYNIAN," 400.
15. Wolters, "IOYNIAN," 401–3.

or a Latin feminine name. Wolter's acceptance should in itself be acknowledged. For him, the answer depends upon how one judges the likelihood that Paul would describe a woman as "prominent among the apostles." In Wolter's opinion, a "plausible," but "not decisive" case can be made for either judgment.[16]

Nijay Gupta maintains that the focus on Junia's gender and apostleship has distracted us from Paul's mention of her imprisonment. Gupta writes his article to fill this hole in Pauline scholarship. Gupta feels that Paul is referring to a literal imprisonment of Andronicus and Junia, and that it was an imprisonment they shared with Paul in the same place at the same time.[17] They were probably charged with either civil disobedience or inciting a riot. In a phrase, their crime was civil disturbance.[18] Gupta refers to the *Passion of Perpetua and Felicity* (c. 203 CE) as he describes conditions possibly faced by Junia.[19] The conditions were horrific enough for men, and would have been especially horrific for women. Gupta concludes that Junia was imprisoned long enough to earn the label "fellow prisoner," but for a period short enough to survive. In other words, for weeks, not months.[20]

Gupta, nevertheless, revisits the decades-old debate about the gender and apostleship of Junia. That Ἰουνίαν (*Iounian*) is the accusative (direct object) form of the feminine name Ἰουνία (*Iounia*, Junia) is widely affirmed in Pauline scholarship.[21] The early church fathers, listed by Gupta as Origen, Ambrosiaster, Chrysostom, Jerome, Theodoret, John Damascene, Peter Abelard, and Peter Lombard, read *Iounian* as a woman's name. Bernadette Brooten and Eldon Epp observe that there is no literary evidence at all for a masculine name Junias in antiquity.[22] On this basis, there is widespread conviction that Paul referred to a woman named Junia in Rom 16:7,

---

16. Wolters, "IOYNIAN," 408n70.
17. Gupta, "Reconstructing Junia's Imprisonment," 390.
18. Gupta, "Reconstructing Junia's Imprisonment," 391, 395.
19. Gupta, "Reconstructing Junia's Imprisonment," 394.
20. Gupta, "Reconstructing Junia's Imprisonment," 396.
21. Gupta, "Reconstructing Junia's Imprisonment," 385, 387.
22. Gupta, "Reconstructing Junia's Imprisonment," 386.

and as Gupta observes, this is reflected in English translations like the NRSV, NIV, NET, and NAB. As Gupta further says, "This now appears to be a foregone conclusion in 21st century scholarship on early Christianity."[23]

There is still debate about Junia and Andronicus' relationship to the apostles. Were they "noteworthy to the apostles," which would mean that they themselves were not being called apostles, or were they "prominent among the apostles," which would mean that they themselves were also apostles.[24]

Gupta compares the statistical study of Michael Burer and Daniel Wallace to Richard Bauckham's study of gospel women. Burer and Wallace concluded that ἐπίσημοι + ἐν (*episēmoi + en*) + dative (indirect object) was mostly exclusive, which means that Paul did not include Andronicus and Junia among the apostles.[25] Bauckham, however, finds it inconceivable that the early church fathers, all Greek speakers, would be mistaken about Paul's identification of Andronicus and Junia as apostles. Gupta mentions other scholars who question Burer and Wallace's methods, data, and conclusions.[26] Gupta is convinced that Origen provides the most likely meaning of "apostles" as intended in Rom 16:7—as the seventy-two emissaries of Jesus in Luke 10:1.

Yii-Jan Lin rises to analyze counterarguments to Bernadette Brooten, Eldon Epp, and others who hold that a woman named Junia was described as a prominent apostle by Paul in Rom 16:7. She contends that Wolter's attempt to show that Ἰουνίαν, *Iounian* derives from a Hebrew masculine name rather than a Latin feminine name does not consider the name and person of Andronicus.[27] It would sound ridiculous to suggest that the well-attested Greek name Andronicus was derived from a Hebrew name, or even a Hebrew feminine name. Why then should the well-attested feminine

23. Gupta, "Reconstructing Junia's Imprisonment," 581.

24. Gupta, "Reconstructing Junia's Imprisonment," 387.

25. Gupta, "Reconstructing Junia's Imprisonment," 387.

26. Gupta, "Reconstructing Junia's Imprisonment," 387–88. See also Burer and Wallace, "Was Junia Really an Apostle?" 76–78; Bauckham, *Gospel Women*.

27. Lin, "Junia," 193.

name Junia be thought to be derived from a Hebrew masculine name? Lin argues that Junia is a Jewish woman with a well-attested Latin feminine name. Lin asks, "Would this not make even better sense considering that IOYNIAN resides in Rome, a city with over 250 Greek and Latin inscriptions with the name 'Junia'?"[28]

Lin next addresses the work of Michael Burer who accepts IOUNIAN as a feminine name, but denies that the woman so named was an apostle.[29] She was only well-known to the apostles—an exclusive sense of *episēmoi*. Burer presents seventy-one new texts that show that Paul could have used *episēmos* + the genitive (possessive) to show that Andronicus and Junia were "among" the apostles. He presents thirty-six new texts which, with the exception of one, are grammatical parallels to Rom 16:7. These texts are meant to prove that Andronicus and Junia were only "well known to the apostles" according to Paul. Burer's argument about a construction that Paul could have used is inconclusive for Lin, and she sets it aside. Lin finds that the thirty-six examples in Burer's second argument are not all exact parallels, and some with "inclusive" meanings are misleadingly translated.[30] Lin finds that Burer is unconvincing.

David Huttar is next in Lin's investigation.[31] Huttar looks in ancient literature for grammatical parallels to Rom 16:7 and finds four. He labels one "inclusive" and the remaining three "non-inclusive." However, according to Lin, he does not consider the scholarship that contradicts his claims.[32] He then seeks to show that the early church fathers interpreted Rom 16:7 "non-inclusively." Lin finds that Huttar's use of the term "non-inclusive" is ambiguous. Moreover, she considers his arguments for "non-inclusive" readings of the early church fathers "convoluted."[33]

---

28. Lin, "Junia," 194.
29. Burer, "ΕΠΙΣΗΜΟΙ," 731–55.
30. Lin, "Junia," 194–96.
31. Huttar, "Did Paul Call Andronicus an Apostle," 747–78.
32. Lin, "Junia," 198n29.
33. Lin, "Junia," 198n30.

TYING IN THE THEME

For Yii-Jan Lin, Huttar's most intriguing argument has to do with "the rhetorical context and force of Rom 16:7."[34] He argues that seeing Andronicus as an apostle does not fit well with the purpose of Paul's greeting. Lin struggles with this observation and concludes that Huttar does not understand the value of rhetorical praise in the Roman setting. Huttar also feels that Paul shows disdain for aligning himself with other apostles, and would be adverse to ranking apostles above other apostles. Lin, however, feels that Paul would not be adverse to aligning apostles to him, and "prominent among the apostles" does not imply ranking.[35]

Lin maintains that the patristic evidence supports Junia as an apostle. In addition, she argues that Gal 1:13—2:10 and 2 Cor 10:12 show that Paul rejects human evaluation of his apostleship. With this general attitude toward human evaluation, Paul is more likely to mention "prominence among the apostles" than "estimation by the apostles."[36] Paul nevertheless praises Andronicus and Junia to strengthen his connection to the Roman church community, and to raise his honor by raising theirs and the honor of the community.[37] By acknowledging their prominence among the apostles, Paul is subtly acknowledging his. Paul's further acknowledgment that Andronicus and Junia were "in Christ before me" only makes sense if Andronicus and Junia are apostles.[38] This is Paul's way of subtly asserting his unique status as the last apostle (1 Cor 15:3-11; Gal 1:11-2:10). By claiming to be the "last and the least," Paul claims to be "first."[39]

These studies of Junia by Wolters, Gupta, and Lin are a small, but representative selection from a vast literary field. In the end, the strength of the case for an apostle named Junia is clearly evident. The discovery of a woman referred to by Paul as an apostle, and as "prominent among the apostles," is not unprecedented in light of

---

34. Lin, "Junia," 199.
35. Lin, "Junia," 200–201.
36. Lin, "Junia," 201–2.
37. Lin, "Junia," 202–3.
38. Lin, "Junia," 204–6.
39. Lin, "Junia," 206–8.

Women, Salvation, and Childbearing

the role assigned by Jesus to Mary Magdalene and a couple of other women (Matt 28:9-10; John 20:17-18). However, the discovery is pivotal for discerning Paul's attitude toward women in the Christian mission.

MARY AND THE REST OF THE WOMEN

Paul otherwise recognizes the leadership and presence of women in the Christian mission on numerous occasions. Beside the women already mentioned in this section, Paul also acknowledges Mary, who "labored greatly among you" (ἥτις πολλὰ ἐκοπίασεν εἰς ὑμᾶς, *hētis polla ekopiasen eis hymas*) (Rom 16:6), Tryphena and Tryphosa, "who labored in the Lord" (τὰς κοπιώσας ἐν κυρίῳ, *tas kopiōsas en kyriō* (Rom 16:12), and Persis, "the beloved, who labored greatly in the Lord" (τὴν ἀγαπητήν, ἥτις πολλὰ ἐκοπίασεν ἐν κυρίῳ, *tēn agapētēn, hētis polla ekopiasen en kyriō;* Rom 16:12). The language is different, but the male Epaphras is also referred to as one who "has labored much" (ἔχει πολὺν πόνον, *echei polyn ponon*) for the churches in Colossae, Laodicea, and Hierapolis (Col 4:13). The women are no less honored for their labor.

Paul also mentions the mother of Rufus, who has also been a mother to Paul (Rom 16:13), Julia (Rom 16:15), the sister of Nereus (Rom 16:15), and Claudia (2 Tim 4:21). These are people who were marginalized in that culture, but not in the heart of Paul. Paul's acknowledgement of them is remarkably counter-cultural.

Special mention is made of Euodia and Syntyche (Phil 4:2), "who fought alongside me in the gospel" (αἵτινες ἐν τῷ εὐαγγελίῳ συνήθλησάν μοι, *haitines en tō euangeliō synēthlēsan moi*) (Phil 4:3). Many people fought alongside Paul in the gospel, but only the women Euodia and Syntyche are singled out for this recognition. The image of Euodia and Syntyche fighting alongside Paul is no less provocative than that of Junia as a fellow-prisoner of Paul or Prisca risking her life for Paul.

Throughout the Pauline corpus where Paul refers to women, it is clear that they are subservient to no one in the leadership of the church. This is one of the strongest indicators for Paul's egalitarian

Tying in the Theme

view. It is also one indication of the egalitarian status of women in the first century Christian mission, and especially in Paul's perspective. Paul's practice of acknowledging and including women is consistent with the great declaration he makes in Gal 3:27–28:

> ὅσοι γὰρ εἰς Χριστὸν ἐβαπτίσθητε, Χριστὸν ἐνεδύσασθε. οὐκ ἔνι Ἰουδαῖος οὐδὲ Ἕλλην, οὐκ ἔνι δοῦλος οὐδὲ ἐλεύθερος, οὐκ ἔνι ἄρσεν καὶ θῆλυ. πάντες γὰρ ὑμεῖς εἷς ἐστε ἐν Χριστῷ Ἰησοῦ, *gar eis Christon ebaptisthēte, Christon enedysasthe. ouk eni Ioudaios oude Hellēn, ouk eni doulos oude eleutheros, ouk eni arsen kai thēlu. pantes gap hymeis heis este en Christō Iēsou.*
>
> For whoever is baptized in Christ, has put on Christ. There is neither Jew nor Greek, there is neither slave nor free, there is neither male and female. For we are all one in Christ Jesus.

People misinterpret this passage when they maintain that Paul advocates the erasure of gender and ethnic identity, or gender and ethnic differences.[40] However, they are correct when they maintain that Paul seeks to erase slavery. Galatians 3:28 is about the erasure of social hierarchy—the assignment of superior and inferior status in human relationships. The removal of hierarchy based on gender and ethnicity does not mean the removal of gender and ethnicity, as if that was possible. However, the removal of social hierarchy does indeed mean the removal of slavery because *slavery is social hierarchy*. The dichotomies of Gal 3:28 are symmetrical, but not parallel. We must not assume that the same end is implied for each binary. The erasure of slavery in this verse does not also mean the erasure of gender and ethnicity.

SCRIPTURAL STUMBLING BLOCKS TO MINISTRY

First Corinthians 11:3–10, 13–15, and especially 14:34 are a set of texts alongside 1 Tim 2:11–15 that have been stumbling blocks

---

40. See Keener's (*Galatians*, 309–10) response to Betz (*Galatians*, 195–99), who thinks that Paul wants to remove biological differences.

Women, Salvation, and Childbearing

to the ministry and leadership of women in the church. The true rhetorical character of these Scriptures has been veiled by cultural distance between the text and modern readers; and also by the simple fact that the Greek text does not have quotation marks to show when someone other than Paul is speaking. David W. Odell-Scott has been instrumental is pulling this veil away. His work certainly deserves more attention than it has received. Odell-Scott has shown that this passage is actually Paul quoting one or more opponents whom he summarily debunks.[41] Odell-Scott has shown this through marking out the dialogue in a way that clearly shows when Paul is speaking and when someone other than Paul is speaking.

The following rhetorical layout is based upon and adapted from Odell-Scott's scholarship. Although I hope that Odell-Scott would agree with this application of this insight, I am not saying that he does. The word concerning the degree to which he agrees or disagrees with the following will have to come from him.[42] It is nevertheless his scholarship that I am drawing upon.

> *The Corinthian opponents say*: "But I want you to know that the head of every man is Christ, the head of the woman is man, and the head of Christ is God. Any man who prays or prophesies with his head covered dishonors his head, but any woman who prays or prophesies with her head uncovered dishonors her head—it is the same as if her head were shaven. For if a woman will not cover herself, then she should cut off her hair; but if it is disgraceful for a woman to be shorn or shaven, let her

---

41. In many contexts, 1 Tim 2:11–15 is often discussed in conjunction with 1 Cor 14:34–35. The two passages combined have posed extreme difficulty for Pauline scholarship. A convincing treatment of this Corinthian passage was presented by Odell-Scott in an unpublished SBL paper entitled "The Paulinist Reversal of Paul's Critique of Gender Subordination." In this paper Odell-Scott demonstrated that 1 Cor 14:34–35 along with 1 Cor 11:3–9, 13–15 are not the words of Paul, but the words of Corinthian opponents whom Paul quotes and then debunks in 1 Cor 11:11–12, 16; 14:36. See also his "Let the Women Speak in Church," and "In Defense of an Egalitarian Interpretation of 1 Cor 14:34–36." In this last article Odell-Scott responds to Murphy-O'Connor, "Interpolations in 1 Corinthians."

42. However, Odell-Scott and I have exchanged communications over our respective work on 1 Cor and 1 Tim.

cover herself. For A man ought not to cover his head, since he is the image and glory of God; but woman is the glory of man. For man was not made from woman, but woman from man. Neither was man created for woman, but woman for man. That is why a woman ought to have authority [ἐξουσίαν, *exousian*] on her head, because of the angels" (1 Cor 11:3–10).

But Paul says in response: "Nevertheless, in the Lord woman is not independent of man, nor man independent of woman; for as woman was made from man, so man is now born of woman. And all things are from God" (1 Cor 11:11–12).

The Corinthian opponents say: "Judge for yourselves: is it proper for a woman to pray to God with her head uncovered? Does not nature herself teach you that for a man to wear long hair is demeaning to him, but if a woman has long hair, it is her glory? For her hair is given to her for a covering" (1 Cor 11:13–15).

But Paul says in response: "If anyone is inclined to be contentious, we have no such practice—neither do the churches of God" (1 Cor 11:16).

The Corinthian opponents say: "Let the women keep silent in the churches. They are not allowed to speak, but let them be submissive, as the law says. If they want to know about something, let them ask their own husbands at home; for it is a shame for a woman to speak in the church" (1 Cor 14:34–35).

But Paul says in response: "What! Did the word of God originate with you (men)? Are you the only ones it has reached?" (1 Cor 14:36)[43]

---

43. Odell-Scott ("Let the Women Speak in Church," 90, 91–93) explains that the particle ē (ἤ) at the beginning of 1 Cor 14:36 fulfills a disjunctive function, and sets up the preceding statement for rebuttal. The exclamation "What!" becomes the best rendering of the disjunctive response. This translation of ē is preserved in the RSV.

Women, Salvation, and Childbearing

In 1 Cor 11:3–16; 14:34–36; and in other places like 1 Cor 8:1–3; 10:23, Paul is using a Greco-Roman rhetorical technique known as *prosōpopoeia* (προσωποποιία, impersonation, personification, dramatization, speech-in-character).[44] It is a technique he frequently uses in his Roman and Corinthian correspondence.[45] Because the Greek text of the New Testament does not have quotation marks, and because many modern readers are not familiar with this technique, Paul's thought in the Roman and Corinthian letters is widely misinterpreted.

The Roman rhetorician Quintilian (35–95 CE) defines *prosōpopoeia* as "fictitious speech of other persons" (*Inst.* 6.1.25).[46] However, Hermogenes of Tarsus (second century CE) will later draw a distinction between *prosōpopoeia* and *ēthopoeia* (ἠθοποιία). He said, "in ethopoeia we imagine words for a real person, in prosopopoeia we imagine a non-existing person (*Prog.* 9).[47] Quintilian did not make this distinction, and *prosōpopoeia* remains as the term that is most frequently used to describe this rhetorical maneuver. In the Greco-Roman world this technique was used in theatre, legal disputes, oratory, and letter writing. It was also used when letters, like the ones Paul wrote, were read to the community. The delegated reader would indicate changes from one speaker to the other through voice inflections, body gestures, posturing, and facial expressions.[48] Paul's first century audience had an advantage we do not have today for distinguishing between Paul's words and the words of the opponents he debunks.

The Corinthian opponents simply do not sound like Paul. This is further indication that Paul is responding to contrary voices. Moreover, the contrary voices appear to be grounded in a pagan religious perspective.

44. Waters, "Paul and Predestination," 49–53.

45. Odell-Scott does not use the term *prosōpopoeia*, in the works cited here, but he gives us the best demonstration of it in the Corinthian letters.

46. Butler, *Institutio Oratoria*.

47. Kennedy, *Prog.*, 84.

48. Cf. Hurtado, "The Gospel of Mark," 17: "In addition, most texts of Greco-Roman antiquity were prepared to be 'performed' before a group, read aloud, with all the techniques of oral communication available to the reader."

TYING IN THE THEME

In the second century novel of Apuleius we have an account of homage paid to the goddess Isis in the city of Cenchreae "which is well-known as part of the illustrious territory of the Corinthians, and is washed by the Aegean Sea and Saronic Gulf" (*Metam.* 10.35).[49] In this novel, the main character Lucius, who had been magically turned into a donkey, is instructed by the goddess Isis to join himself to a procession in her honor. The description of male and female dress in this Corinthian context among the goddess initiates is strongly reminiscence of the debate in 1 Cor 11:3–16.

> Then the crowd of those initiated into the divine mysteries came pouring in, men and women of every rank and age. They shone with the pure radiance of their linen robes; the women's hair was anointed and wrapped in transparent covering, while the men's heads were completely shaven and their skulls gleaned brightly—earthly stars of the great religion. All together made a shrill ringing sound with their sistrums of bronze and silver, and even gold. (*Metam.* 11.10)[50]

In this account we also have a context for understanding Paul's reference to "a banging brass and clanging cymbal" in 1 Cor 13:1.[51] Apuleius's work is a novel, but there is little doubt that his description of Isis veneration in Corinth is grounded in actual practice reaching back before his time. The opponents whom Paul debunks in 1 Cor 11:3–16 and 14:34 seem to be influenced by this kind of practice.

In 1 Cor 11:10, a requirement for covering (or placing "authority" over) the heads of women is justified by debaters "because of the angels." Scholars have travelled various trails in search of a key that would unlock the meaning of this remark. This passage

---

49. Hanson, *Apuleius*, 237.

50. Hanson, *Apuleius*, 255.

51. See the translation of Graves, *The Golden Ass*, 269: "Then followed a great crowd of the Goddess's initiates, men and women of all classes and every age, their pure white linen clothes shining brightly. The women wore their hair tied up in glossy coils under gauze head-dresses; the men's heads were completely shaven, representing the Goddess's bright earthly stars, and they carried rattles of brass, silver and even gold, which kept up a shrill and ceaseless tinkling."

could reflect a legend that the world was not created directly by God, but by the angels. This in turn could indicate a belief that the angels preside over a creation order that requires the subordination of women to men. In the distorted, convoluted mythology of the Gnostic texts, we have echoes of a belief that angels were responsible for the creation of the world:

> Like that of all else is the creation of mankind as well. The spiritual Logos moved him invisibly, as he perfected him through the Demiurge and his angelic servants, who shared in the act of fashioning in [multitudes, when he] took counsel with his archons. (*Tri. Trac.* 104–5)[52]

This text is from the third century CE, but it may carry over themes from earlier forms of Gnosticism (1 Cor 8:1; 1 Tim 6:20; 1 John 4:2–3; 2 John 7).

Further evidence for this angelic theme and its influence upon the Corinthian congregation may also appear in a third century pseudepigraphal letter sent to Paul by a group of Corinthian elders:

> Two men are come to Corinth, named Simon and Cleobius, who pervert the faith of many through pernicious words, which thou shalt put to the test. For never have we heard such words, either from thee or from other [apostles], but what we have received from thee and from them, that we hold fast. . . . What they say and teach is as follows: We must not, they say, appeal to the prophets, and that God is not almighty, and that there is no resurrection of the flesh, and that the creation of man is not God's work, and that the Lord is not come in the flesh, nor was he born of Mary, and that the world is not of God, but of the angels. (3 Cor 1.2–15)[53]

The passage (1 Cor 11:10) could also be a cryptic reference to Gen 6:1–4 and 1 En 6:1–8; 7:1–6; 8:1–4 (cf. 2 Pet 2:4; Jude 6), suggesting that the veil on women's heads was needed to shield them from the attention of disobedient, lustful male angels. These remarks could also indicate human worship of angels, or at least the

---

52. Attridge et al., "The Tripartite Tractate," 87.
53. Schneemelcher and Wilson, *NTA*, 2:254.

Tying in the Theme

belief that angels somehow participate in or preside over worship in human settings. In this case, the covering over women's heads would be a requirement imposed by angels upon women in worship. There are a variety of other proposals for understanding this verse.[54] However, the most critical point in the interpretation of 1 Cor 11:10 is almost always missed by scholars, namely, that this verse does not reflect the thinking of Paul the Apostle, but only opponents whom Paul debunks. Paul in 1 Cor 11:1–16 and 14:34–36 is engaging a Corinthian opposition that is influenced by pagan and heretical religious beliefs. It is true that Paul authored the words in these pericopes, but he did it as rhetorical ploy to undercut an opposing view.

THE OTHER SIDE OF THE DEBATE

My conclusions about Paul and women are a radical departure from the judgements of other scholars. Elisabeth Schüssler Fiorenza rightly discerns from Paul's references that women are prominent leaders and missionaries in the first century Christian mission, of which they are also wealthy patrons. As Jewish Christian missionaries they may have belonged to the Christian communities in Galilee, Jerusalem, and Antioch from the very beginnings of Christianity. They both preceded Paul and are independent of him. In the ministry, they are Paul's equal and some may even be his superior.[55] However, Schüssler Fiorenza also maintains that Paul's struggles with this state of affairs. She observes that the "pre-Pauline baptismal formula" in Gal 3:28 removed all hierarchical religious and social prerogatives, particularly those involving ethnicity, gender, and slavery. Nevertheless, she argues, we see a departure from this egalitarianism in "later gnostic and patristic writings."[56] Paul himself made alterations to the tradition preserved in Gal 3:28.

---

54. See Stuckenbruck, "Why Should Women Cover," 205–34 for a wide range of options. However, Stuckenbruck himself believes that "1 Cor 11:2–16 is Pauline" (218).

55. Schüssler Fiorenza, *In Memory of Her*, 161.

56. Schüssler Fiorenza, *In Memory of Her*, 217–18.

Women, Salvation, and Childbearing

These alterations lead into the direction of this departure from egalitarianism. Notably, in 1 Cor 12:13, where Paul quotes Gal 3:28, the male and female dichotomy is omitted.[57]

In the Corinthian correspondence Schüssler Fiorenza sees more evidence of Paul's dissociation of himself from the egalitarian practices of the early church. Schüssler Fiorenza observes that 1 Cor 14:33b–36 may be an editorial interpolation, but since these verses cannot be excluded on text-critical grounds, it is more exegetically sound to treat them as original. Schüssler Fiorenza therefore understands Paul's sanctions upon women as a means of controlling "orgiastic behavior" in the worshipping community. In so doing, Paul introduces "patriarchal imagery and language."[58] Schüssler Fiorenza acknowledges that Paul's incorporation of the Gal 3:28 baptismal formula in his dialogue with the Corinthians is affirmation of female equality and spiritual giftedness in the church; however, Paul proceeds to mark out a distinction between married and unmarried women in the Christian mission. Married women, in his perspective, are encumbered with the cares of this world, while unmarried women ascend to a higher level of freedom and spirituality. Married women in the Christian community become heavily hindered in this circumstance. Schüssler Fiorenza describes Paul's impact upon women's leadership in the Christian mission as "double-edged." At one point he affirms women's equality and freedom in mission and ministry, at another point Paul slips back into patriarchal subordination of women.[59] It then becomes worse as the legacy of Paul is passed down. As Schüssler Fiorenza observes:

> The post-Pauline and pseudo-Pauline tradition will draw out these restrictions in order to change the equality in Christ between women and men, slaves and free, into a relationship of subordination in the household which, on the one hand, eliminates women from the leadership of worship and community and, on the other restricts their ministry to women.[60]

57. Schüssler Fiorenza, *In Memory of Her*, 219.
58. Schüssler Fiorenza, *In Memory of Her*, 233.
59. Schüssler Fiorenza, *In Memory of Her*, 235–36.
60. Schüssler Fiorenza, *In Memory of Her*, 236.

Tying in the Theme

Rosemary Radford Ruether also does not believe that the baptismal theology of Gal 3:28 originated with Paul. She believes it was pre-Pauline, but closely associated with the Hellenistic Christian mission that Paul joined.[61] She denies that Paul created the formula because Paul did not promote "pre-fallen wholeness" nor the "social equality of women with men, slaves with masters, that would allow either women or slaves to throw off their subordination to the paterfamilias of the household."[62] In the Corinthian letters, Ruether sees Paul refuting Corinthian beliefs and practices that dissolved hierarchical relations between women and men, and between people of different classes.[63] First Timothy, according to Ruether, is a second-century pseudonymous letter that represents the conflict between two versions of Pauline Christianity, a patriarchal version which subordinates women, and a version which promotes spiritual equality for women. The first version became "orthodox," and was canonized in the NT. The second version became "relegated to the fringes and transmuted into various forms."[64]

Schüssler Fiorenza and Ruether provide full-length, detailed, and meticulously documented arguments for a rather patriarchal-minded Paul. A point-by-point response to their presentation cannot be fitted into these pages. However, we must at least observe that their characterizations of Paul the Apostle fail to take account of Paul's rhetorical practices and strategies. Consequently, they misread Paul at critical points, particularly in regard to his attitude toward women. A case in point is their discussion of Gal 3:28.

Whether or not Gal 3:28 is a baptismal formula, and whether or not the verse originated with Paul, it was still incorporated into Paul's thought and illustrated by his practice. The verse expresses the *oneness* of *all* in Christ, and the removal of hierarchical relationships. The message is different in 1 Cor 12:13. This verse expresses the *oneness* of the body of Christ itself, and its inclusive membership. There is no question that both women are men are included

---

61. Ruether, *Women and Redemption*, 24.
62. Ruether, *Women and Redemption*, 25.
63. Ruether, *Women and Redemption*, 27.
64. Ruether, *Women and Redemption*, 31–32.

Women, Salvation, and Childbearing

in the body. Even the opponents of Paul in 1 Cor 11:3–16 acknowledge that women are present in the body of Christ, and that they active in the ministry of prayer and prophecy. These opponents object to women praying and prophesying with uncovered heads; and they object to women speaking in church, but they seem to be a minority faction. Moreover, the leadership role of Chloe in particular is strongly implied (1 Cor 1:11). The leadership and presence of women in the church is not an issue for the majority. However, there is the question of whether Greeks must become Jews to be included in the body of Christ (1 Cor 7:17–20), and whether slaves must become free in order to be included (1 Cor 7:21–24). Paul addresses these questions by affirming that *all* of us are included by the spirit in the body of Christ whether Jew or Greek, slave or free. The dichotomy of male and female is not included in 1 Cor 12:13 because the inclusion of women in the body of Christ is not questioned by the majority of members in Corinth. The same could be said of Col 3:11 where we have another statement of contrasting demographics in unity.[65] While there are references to "Greek and Jew, circumcised and uncircumcised, barbarian, Scythian, slave and free" in Col 3:11 there is no reference to female and male. But the reference is not necessary. The acknowledgement of "Nympha and the church in her house" (Col 4:15), and Apphia, who seems to co-host a church in her house (Phlm 2), are indicators that the pastoral leadership of women is a well-established institution in Colossae and Laodicea. In 1 Cor 12:13 and Col 3:11, Paul is not altering the tradition preserved in Gal 3:28 in order to suppress women. He is focusing his attention upon the actual issues at hand, the inclusion of Gentiles and slaves in the body of Christ.

However, some would point out that there are no indications of an issue involving women in Paul's letter to the Galatians. Yet he makes a statement in Gal 3:28 that affirms the inclusion and equality of women in Christ. This is taken as an indication that Gal 3:28 is a pre-Pauline baptismal formula.[66] There are reasons to call these observations into question. For Paul to say, "For in Christ Jesus

---

65. See Wright, *Paul*, 56–61. Notably, Wright argues for the Pauline authorship of the Letter to the Colossians.

66. Cf. Hays, "Galatians," 273.

Tying in the Theme

neither circumcision nor uncircumcision accomplishes anything" (Gal 5:6), is also to say "neither does being male accomplish anything." Paul is speaking in reference to salvation. If male circumcision is the key to salvation than that automatically consigns women to a subordinate role. Their salvation at best becomes dependent upon their relationship to a circumcised male. It is only in this way that women also become children of Abraham. Yet Paul's message is that "You know then that it is those of faith who are children of Abraham" (Γινώσκετε ἄρα ὅτι οἱ ἐκ πίστεως, οὗτοι υἱοί εἰσιν Ἀβραάμ, *Ginōskete ara hoti hoi ek pisteōs, houtoi huioi eisin Abraam*) (Gal 3:7). Despite the RSV, the term "men of faith" (οἱ ἄνδρες ἐκ πίστεως, *hoi andres ek pisteōs*) does not appear in this verse. The more inclusive "those of faith" appears, and the term υἱοί, *huioi*, which is sometime translated "sons," has instead the more inclusive sense of "children" in this context and many others (Rom 9:26–27, 2 Cor 3:7, 13; Gal 3:26; Eph 2:2; 5:6; Col 3:6; 1 Thess 5:5). In Gal 3:29, Paul says, "if you are of Christ, then you are the children of Abraham, and heirs according to the promise" (εἰ δὲ ὑμεῖς Χριστοῦ ἄρα τοῦ Ἀβραάμ σπέρμα ἐστέ, κατ' ἐπαγγελίαν κληρονόμοι, *ei de hymeis Christou ara tou Abraam sperma este, kat' epangelian klēronomoi*). It is clear that σπέρμα, *sperma* (seed, offspring, children) in Gal 3:29 is interchangeable with *huioi* in Gal 3:26 and other places. Since this verse follows Gal 3:28, it is undeniable that *sperma* includes "male and female." Since Gal 3:26 precedes Gal 3:28, it is undeniable that *huioi* includes "male and female." The term *huioi* is best translated "children" in Galatians because it includes male and female, and intentionally so. Paul does seem to be responding to an issue involving the exclusion and subordination of women in Galatia after all.

Moreover, with his use of female imagery in Galatians, Paul seems bent on dismantling a patriarchal mindset in the letter's recipients. Paul says that "when God, who separated me from my mother's womb (ὁ ἀφορίσας με ἐκ κοιλίας μητρός μου, *ho aphorisas me ek koilias mētros mou*) and called me through his grace, was pleased to reveal his son to me.... I did not confer with flesh and blood" (Gal 1:15–16). Paul said this to establish his independence from the Jerusalem apostles. When Paul speaks in other correspondence of how God has worked in him (1 Cor 15:3–11; 1 Tim 1:12–17), he makes no mention of his mother, not even as an aside as he does here. This oblique mention of his mother in Galatians would seem innocuous if not for the other female images evoked by Paul in this letter. It may be that Paul alludes to his mother as one way of honoring female presence in God's missional plan.

Paul also mentions that Jesus is "born of a woman" in Gal 4:4. Elsewhere he speaks of Jesus as "descended from David" (Rom 1:3; 2 Tim 2:8). Why does Paul replace this messianic genealogy with a maternal one in Galatians? Is he trying to make a point?

Paul even likens himself to a pregnant woman about to give birth to children (Gal 4:19). Elsewhere Paul describes himself as a father (1 Cor 4:15). Why does Paul apply such an incongruous metaphor to himself in Galatians? Furthermore, in Gal 4:19, it is Paul's expectation that the Galatian believers themselves would become *pregnant* with Christ. It is as if Paul is subtly attacking some unidentified form of hypermasculinity. If so, Paul is not trying to erase gender difference; he is trying to overthrow gender hierarchy and subordination of women.

In Gal 4:21–31, Sarah and Hagar respectively become the mothers of Freedom and Bondage. Paul does not use this female allegorical imagery in Romans 4 where he also speaks of the children of Abraham. He must have a special reason for using it in Galatians.

Most of Paul's references to Jerusalem are straightforward and mundane (Rom 15:19, 25, 26, 31; 1 Cor 16:3; Gal 1:17, 18; 2:1). In these references, Jerusalem is only a destination; but in Gal 4:25–26, Paul distinguishes between the present Jerusalem and the "Jerusalem above." In both references he uses female imagery. The present Jerusalem is in slavery with "her children." The "Jerusalem above" is free and "she is our mother." In Gal 4:27, Paul furthermore draws upon Isa 54:1 for an image of Jerusalem as a married and then desolate woman. Although this language is an extension of his Sarah and Hagar allegory, he did not have to use it. Furthermore, his application appears rather forced and awkward. What motivated Paul to make the application at all?

Tying in the Theme

Added to these, Paul includes a "male and female" binary in a unity statement (Gal 3:28). As we have seen, he does not use a male and female binary elsewhere in other unity statements (1 Cor 12:13; Col 3:11).

Why these shifts in language to the use of female imagery in Galatians? It may be an indication of Paul's sensitivity to the suppression of women in Galatia. In this case, Gal 3:28 may not be a pre-Pauline baptismal formula after all. It may be a creed that originates with Paul. The male and female theme may be intentionally asserted by Paul to affirm women in the church. At the very least, this high concentration of female imagery in Galatians are not absent-minded, casual expressions of Paul. They are intentional responses to something in the Galatian mindscape.

The matter of Paul's attitude toward married women in the Christian mission has also been raised. Here we seem to have another case of misinterpreting Paul. Schüssler Fiorenza provides an ironic staging of the issue:

> Paul's theological argument, however, that those who marry are "divided" and not equally dedicated to the affairs of the Lord as the nonmarried, implicitly limited married women to the confines of the patriarchal family.... One can only wonder how Paul could have made such a theological point when he had Prisca as his friend and knew other missionary couples who were living examples that his theology was wrong.[67]

It is true that this is exactly what one would wonder if Paul's statement in 1 Cor 7:32–35 was meant to "limit married women to the confines of the patriarchal family." However, Paul's statement in these verses was not meant to limit married women in this way. Paul's only intent was to warn that "those who marry will have worldly troubles" (1 Cor 7:28). This does not mean that Paul wanted to restrict married women to the household, no more than it meant that Paul wanted to restrict married men to the household. Paul thought that given the shortness of time it was better to remain unmarried and unencumbered by family affairs, but at

---

67. Schüssler Fiorenza, *In Memory of Her*, 226.

the same time Paul made it clear that he was not opposed to marriage (1 Cor 7:26–31). Nor was Paul opposed to married people in ministry (Rom 16:3; 1 Cor 9:5). When it comes to discerning Paul's attitude toward women in the Christian mission, both married and unmarried, it is critical that we pay attention to both his words and practice.

It should still be acknowledged that the scholarship of Schüssler Fiorenza, Ruether, and other feminist scholars is a needed challenge and refutation of patriarchal bias in biblical hermeneutics and Christian theology. The feminist critique of patriarchy is an important movement in biblical and theological studies as well as in other disciplines, and this movement must be sustained. However, there is room for critique even within the critique. The judgement that Paul is patriarchal, chauvinistic, or misogynistic overlooks his egalitarian practices and language, including the rhetorical features of his thought. Paul is an ally for those who affirm the calling of women to ministry and leadership in the church. We need to more clearly hear his voice.

My purpose in this chapter has been to show that the egalitarian portrait of Paul that emerges from my allegorical reading of 1 Tim 2:11–15, and particularly from my metaphorical interpretation of "childbearing" in 1 Tim 2:15, is both consistent and coherent with the portrait of Paul that emerges from an overall reading of the Pauline letters. This portrait, however, requires attention to Paul's rhetorical practices and strategies, such as the use of allegory, metaphor, and *prosōpopoeia*, on the one hand, and the egalitarian praise and support of his female co-workers on the other. Otherwise, we consign ourselves to a superficial, surface reading of the biblical text, and that would ultimately be misleading.

6

Affirming the Author
The Undying Debate

AUTHORSHIP OR PSEUDONYMITY

In my discussion of 1 Tim 2:11–15 in the previous chapters, I did not spend time on the question of the authorship of the Pastoral Epistles. It would have been a digression from my main theme, and it was not a necessary question to resolve for the purposes of my argument. It is nevertheless an important question, and one that can be appropriately addressed here. Was Paul of Tarsus actually the author of 1 Timothy, 2 Timothy, and Titus?[1] There are those who would affirm Paul's authorship of these letters, and those who would deny it. There are those who would say that the Pauline authorship of the Pastorals Epistles cannot be proven. However, it can also be said that the Pauline authorship of the Pastoral Epistles cannot be disproven. Much depends upon the mindset with which an interpreter approaches the Pastoral Epistles. With that said, I will

---

1. Again, many scholars presuppose that 1 Timothy, 2 Timothy, and Titus were at least produced by the same writer. See Fitzmyer, "The Structured Ministry of the Church," 583; Ramelli, "The Pastoral Epistles and Hellenistic Philosophy," 567–69, 575.

proceed to show in what sense I think Paul is indeed the author of these letters.

The author of the Pastoral Epistles identifies himself as Paul the Apostle (1 Tim 1:1; 2 Tim 1:1; Titus 1:1). Either the author is Paul or he is a pseudonymous author writing after the deaths of Paul, Timothy, Titus, Demas, Crescens, Luke, Mark, Carpus, Alexander, Prisca, Aquila, the household of Onesiphorus, Erastus, Trophimus, Eubulus, Pedens, Linus, Claudia, Artemas, Tychicus, Zenas, Apollos, their families, their descendants, their associates, and anyone else who would have knowledge and memory of the real Paul and these persons mentioned in the letters. These three letters would be passed off to a congregation as "recently discovered" letters of Paul to Timothy and Titus, but the current recipients at that time would be persons cut off from the living memory of everyone mentioned in these letters, and even from the memory of someone like Nero and members of his court (Phil 1:13; 4:22) who are present in the background (Titus 3:1; 2 Tim 4:6), but not mentioned in the letters. These would therefore be letters composed in the second century at the earliest; and the recipients at that time would be somewhere other than Ephesus and Crete. Only under these circumstances could these letters be accepted as authentic in a church culture that knew Paul's writings (2 Cor 10:9–10; 2 Peter 3:15–16) and that were alert to forgeries (Rom 16:22; 1 Cor 16:21; Gal 6:11; Col 4:18; 2 Thess 2:2–3; 3:17; Phlm 19).

It was also customary in that day that the authorship and authenticity of a letter would be confirmed by the letter carrier who was also the public reader of the letter (Rom 16:1; Phil 2:25; 1 Thess 5:27; Col 4:7, 9, 16; Phlm 12 would be an exception to the public reader role).[2] The implication would be that these letters were once sent to Ephesus and Crete (1 Tim 1:3; 2 Tim 1:18; Titus 1:5), where they would have been read, and most likely copied, and distributed. However, if these are really pseudonymous letters there would be no record or memory of these letters arriving in these places. There would also be no record or memory in Ephesus and Crete of the circumstances that were being addressed in these letters.

---

2. See Johnson, "Paul's Letters Reheard," 60–76. See also Laird, "Early Titles of the Pauline Letters," 175.

Furthermore, no one living in the places of the actual destinations of these letters would have ever travelled to Ephesus or Crete to verify the purported history and content of these letters. Further still, no one from Ephesus or Crete would have ever come to the actual destinations of these letters to either confirm or disconfirm their purported history and content. The actual recipients of these letters would have to had been extremely cut-off from the rest of the Mediterranean world for these letters to not be exposed as non-Pauline. At this point, it is very hard to see how these pseudonymous letters could have passed as authentic letters of Paul within the back and forth travelling network of Christian missionaries in the Mediterranean world even in the second century. In comparison, the authenticity of the *Shepherd of Hermas* was questioned in the second and third centuries, and eventually denied a place in the New Testament canon.[3]

STYLE AND SUBSTANCE

The author of the Pastoral Epistles makes brief autobiographical statements (1 Tim 1:12–17; 2 Tim 1:15–18; 3:10–11; 4:6–17; Titus 3:12). If this was someone pretending to be Paul his only purpose for doing so would be to convince the addressees of the letters' authenticity. Why then does he provide them so little autobiographical information? It is understandable that the real Paul writing to actual missionary partners like Timothy and Titus would not provide much in the way of autobiographical details. There is no need. We would expect a pretender to put forth greater effort to convince. The appearance of providing autobiographical information, would be an attempt at convincing an audience that this is really Paul writing. Supposedly, the more information the better. The dearth of autobiography in the Pastoral Epistles is simply not consistent with someone trying to convince others that he is someone he is not. The Pastoral Epistles have the feel of someone who has a close relationship with the original recipients. Timothy, Titus, and their congregational hearers are sure of the sender's identity.

3. Holmes, *The Apostolic Fathers*, 329–31.

Women, Salvation, and Childbearing

The author shows close, personal knowledge of the primary recipients (1 Tim 1:2–3, 18; 4:12; 5:23; 2 Tim 1:2, 5; 3:10–17; Titus 1:4–5). Especially in the case of Timothy, Paul shows intimate knowledge of family, upbringing, health issues, ordination, and church setting. Paul uses endearing terms for both Timothy and Titus. The personal nature of this correspondence is difficult to explain on the theory of pseudonymous authorship. This aspect of the Pastorals poses the most formidable challenge to this theory. It is furthermore not likely that a pretender would fabricate letters directly addressing individuals rather than the whole congregation. Personal connections evoke a web of relationships that range far and wide. Even in that era, it would not be an insurmountable challenge to verify whether there was a bishop Timothy in Ephesus and a bishop Titus in Crete who received a letter from Paul the Apostle within a few years before his death. Members of those congregations along with individuals in the network at large would even be able to provide information about the arrival of these letters in their communities including the name of the letter carrier. A pretender would not leave nor be able to leave such a trail of intimate details. Too many avenues of verifiability would be opened up. We must ask why were these letters accepted and cherished as letters of Paul. They had to have more going for them than the claims of a pseudonymous author.

Those who argue against Paul's authorship of the Pastoral Epistles do so on the basis of differences in vocabulary and writing style between these letters and the undisputed letters. They point out that major Pauline themes are absent. Moreover, they will observe that pseudonymous authorship was common practice in that time. These are issues that should be taken seriously. Accordingly, recent scholarship on Paul and his literary environment has summoned us to rethink the whole practice of ancient letter writing.

David Capes, Rodney Reeves, and E. Randolph Richards challenge the whole notion of a solitary writer composing a letter to one or more recipients in the ancient world. "Paul's letters were communal products, not the work of a single mind. Secretaries and co-authors exercised an influence over the composition of these letters."[4] These three scholars describe a process where Paul and one or more colleagues would hire a secretary to compose a letter. The process was more discussion with the secretary than dictation. This was because the dictation process would be too slow.[5] The secretary would reproduce thoughts and ideas on a wax tablet or parchment in dialogue with the customer. There may be actual "dictation" of brief sections. The result would be rough draft from which the secretary would compose a polished letter.[6] Paul would be the authority behind the letter. His name would be on the letter, and he would be the one held accountable. Nevertheless, the letter was a community composition consisting of preformed traditions and team input.[7] Variations in style and vocabulary would naturally result from the contributions of different individuals and secretaries.[8] Capes, Reeves, and Richards are not convinced that differences in style and vocabulary are sufficient grounds for judging a letter as pseudonymous[9].

This broadens our understanding of Pauline authorship, and explains how the Pastoral Epistles can be authentic letters of Paul despite differences in style and vocabulary from letters like Romans and Galatians. I would add another mitigating factor, namely, the stressful, hectic pace of missionary travels, and the further stress of imprisonment. At the time of 1 Timothy and Titus, Paul seems to be in Macedonia (1 Tim 1:3; Titus 1:5). At the time of 2 Timothy, he seems to be imprisoned in Rome (2 Tim 1:16–17; 4:16–17). Under these circumstances it is very probable that Paul would be conveying his message to a traveling companion, while actually on the road or in prison. The traveling companion would make notes, and then at a later stage compose the letters to be sent to Timothy and Titus in the name of Paul. These would not be dictated letters;

---

4. Capes et al., *Rediscovering Paul*, 18–19.
5. Capes et al., *Rediscovering Paul*, 68–73.
6. Capes et al., *Rediscovering Paul*, 70.
7. Capes et al., *Rediscovering Paul*, 73–76.
8. Capes et al., *Rediscovering Paul*, 71–72.
9. Capes et al., *Rediscovering Paul*, 72.

Women, Salvation, and Childbearing

and not really communal letters. They would be "delegated" letters, but letters still bearing the imprint of Paul.

CLEMENT, POLYCARP, AND CHRONOLOGY

Chronology is also important. If these letters were known by church leaders in the first and second century, that would indicate an earlier first century composition. That would be too early for a pseudonymous attempt. A first century authorship for the Pastoral Epistles is indicated by "echoes" of these letters in 1 Clement, a late first century letter from the church in Rome to the church in Corinth. These echoes are best shown by a side by side comparison:

Table 1: Clement and the Pastoral Epistles	
1 Clement	*Pastoral Epistles*
You had no regret at all in doing good, but you were *ready for every good work* (ἕτοιμοι εἰς πᾶς ἔργον ἀγαθόν, *etoimoi eis pas ergon agathon*). (2:7)	Remind them to be subject to rulers, authorities, to be obedient, to be *ready for every good work* (πρὸς πᾶν ἔργον ἀγαθὸν ἑτοίμους εἶναι, *pros pan ergon agathon etoimous einai*). (Titus 3:1)
Let us therefore approach him in holiness of soul *lifting up to him holy and undefiled hands* (ἀγνὰς καὶ ἀμιάντους χεῖρας αἴροντες πρὸς αὐτόν, *hagnas kai amiantous cheiras airontes pros auton*). (29:1)	I wish that men pray in every place *lifting up holy hands* (ἐπαίροντας ὁσίους χεῖρας, *epairontas hosious cheiras*) without anger and quarreling. (1 Tim 2:8)
We have seen that all the righteous *adorn themselves with good works* (ἐν ἔργοις ἀγαθοῖς πάντες ἐκοσμήθησαν οἱ δίκαιοι, *en ergois agathois pantes ekosmēthēsan hoi dikaioi*), and the Lord himself *having adorned himself with good works* (ἔργοις ἀγαθοῖς ἑαυτὸν κοσμήσας ἐχάρη, *ergois agathois eauton kosmēsas echarē*), rejoiced. (33:7)	Likewise, also the women in modest appearance with decency and temperance *adorn themselves* (κοσμεῖν ἑαυτάς, *kosmein eautas*), not with braided hair and gold or pearls or expensive clothes, but what is \proper for women professing godly reverence *with good works* (δι' ἔργων ἀγαθῶν, *di' ergōn agathōn*). (1 Tim 2:9–10)

Give harmony and peace to us and to all those who dwell on the earth, just as you gave it to our fathers when they reverently called upon you *in faith and truth* (ἐν πίστει καὶ ἀληθείᾳ, *en pistei kai alētheia*). (60:4)	For which I was appointed a preacher and apostle, I speak the truth, I lie not, a teacher of the Gentiles *in faith and truth* (ἐν πίστει καὶ ἀληθείᾳ, *en pistei kai alētheia*). (1 Tim 2:7)
For you, heavenly Master, *King of the Ages* (βασιλεῦ τῶν αἰώνων, *basileu tōn aiōnōn*), give to the sons of men glory, and honor, and authority over all those who are on earth. (61.2)	To the *King of the Ages* (βασιλεῖ τῶν αἰώνων, *basilei tōn aiōnōn*), immortal, invisible, the only God, be honor and glory for ever and ever, amen. (1 Tim 1:17)

Notably, both 1 Clem 33:7 and 1 Tim 2:9–10 occur as part of a reflection upon the creation of male and female humanity in the Genesis narrative (1 Clem 33:4–6; 1 Tim 2:13–15).

Many scholars have concluded that 1 Clement was written during the reign of the emperor Domitian. This is largely because Eusebius, drawing upon the historian Hegesippus (c. 110–180 CE), shows that Linus became bishop of Rome in the first year of the emperor Vespasian (69 CE), Anencletus became bishop of Rome in the final year of the emperor Titus (81 CE), and that Clement became bishop of Rome in the twelfth year of the emperor Domitian (93 CE)[10] It was during this time that Domitian intensified his persecution of Jews and Christ followers. The beginning of Clement's letter is often cited to indicate this trial.

> Because of the sudden and repeated misfortunes and reverses which have happened to us, brothers, we acknowledge that we have been somewhat slow in giving attention to the matters in dispute among you, dear friends, especially the detestable and unholy schism, so alien and strange to those chosen by God, which a few reckless and arrogant persons have kindled to such a

---

10. Eusebius, *Hist. eccl.* 3.13–15; 3.21.1; Irenaeus, *Haer.* III.3.3. also testifies to Clement as the third bishop of Rome.

pitch of insanity that your good name, once so renowned and loved by all, has been greatly reviled. (1 Clem 1:1)[11]

Clement's reference to "the sudden and repeated misfortunes and reverses which have happened to us" is frequently taken as reference to the persecutions of Domitian. Clement seems to describe a context of persecution motivated by the kind of jealousy and envy frequently ascribed to Domitian.

> Because of jealousy and envy the greatest and most righteous pillars were persecuted, and fought to the death. (1 Clem 5:2)[12]

Clement values the example of the Apostles and clearly compares the sufferings of his contemporaries to theirs:

> To these men who lived holy lives there was joined a vast multitude of the elect who, having suffered many torments and tortures because of jealousy, set an illustrious example among us. Because of jealousy women were persecuted as Danaids and Dircae, suffering in this way terrible and unholy tortures, but they safely reached the goal in the race of faith, and received a noble reward, their physical weakness notwithstanding. (1 Clem 6:1–2)[13]

It is moreover clear that Clement sees the contemporary sufferings of the church as a continuation of previous persecutions. "For we are in the same arena," he says, "and the same contest awaits us" (1 Clem 7:1).[14] The author of 1 Clement describes Peter and Paul as the "champions nearest in time to us" (ἐπὶ τοὺς ἔγγιστα γενομένους ἀθλητάς, *epi tous engista genomenous athlētas*) and as "those born of our generation" (τῆς γενεᾶς ἡμῶν τὰ γενναῖα, *tēs geneas hēmōn ta gennaia*). The author therefore shows that he is a contemporary of the martyrs Peter and Paul, even if he is not the Clement mentioned by Paul in Phil 4:3.

---

11. Holmes, *The Apostolic Fathers*, 29.
12. Holmes, *The Apostolic Fathers*, 35.
13. Holmes, *The Apostolic Fathers*, 35.
14. Holmes, *The Apostolic Fathers*, 36.

Although he writes at a later time, Polycarp of Smyrna (c. 69–155) provides further support for an early date for the Pastoral Epistles.[15] As with Clement, the evidence for Polycarp's knowledge of these letters appears as "echoes," but in a letter he writes to the Philippians.

Table 2: Polycarp and the Pastoral Epistles

Polycarp, *Phil.*	Pastoral Epistles
But the *love of money* (φιλαργορία, *philargoria*) is the beginning of all troubles. (4:1)	For the *love of money* (ἡ φιλαργορία, *hē philargoria*) is the root of all evils. (1 Tim 6:10)
Knowing, therefore, that *we brought nothing* (οὐδὲν εἰσηνέγκαμεν, *ouden eisēnegkamen*) into the world, nor that we can take anything out. (4:1)	For we brought nothing (οὐδὲν γὰρ εἰσηνέγκαμεν, *ouden gar eisēnegkamen*) into the world, nor can we take anything out. (1 Tim 6:7)
Likewise, deacons must be blameless in the presence of his righteousness, etc. (5:2)	Likewise, deacons must be respectable, etc. (1 Tim 3:8–13)
We shall also reign with him (καὶ συμβασιλεύσομεν, *kai symbasileusomen*), if, that is, we believe. (5:2)	If we endure, *we shall also reign with him* (καὶ συμβασιλεύσομεν, *kai symbasileusomen*). (2 Tim. 2:12)
For they did not love this present age (οὐ γὰρ τὸν νῦν ἠγάπησαν αἰῶνα, *ou gar ton nun ēgapēsan aiōna*). (9:2)	For Demas, *in love with this present age* (ἀγαπήσας τὸν νῦν αἰῶνα, *agapēsas ton nun aiōna*), has forsaken me. (2 Tim 4:10)
If a man cannot govern himself in these matters, how can he require discipline from someone else. (11:2)	If anyone does not know how to manage his own house, how can he take care of the church of God. (1 Tim 3:5)

---

15. Towner (*The Letters to Timothy and Titus*, 4), observes that it is sometimes impossible to tell whether an ancient author is drawing upon these letters or using "common phraseology." "Nevertheless," Towner says, "the evidence from Polycarp (c. 110–35) and 1 Clement (their use of language and casual quotations) suggests strongly that these letters were known and used by these early witnesses. Polycarp's knowledge and use of the Pauline Corpus as a whole further suggest that the letters to Timothy and Titus were regarded as part of that collection."

Women, Salvation, and Childbearing

Polycarp wrote early in the second century (c. 117), and drew upon a collection of letters that included 1 and 2 Timothy. This suggests that the letters of Paul (including 1 and 2 Timothy) were already circulating as a collection as early as the first century.[16] This is already indicated by the use of Paul's letters in the letter of Clement, but Polycarp strengthens the case for the authenticity of the Pastoral Epistles.[17] For Polycarp, the letters of Paul were Sacred Scripture (*sacris literis*, *Phil.* 12.1). They were part of the "word delivered to us from the beginning" (*Phil.* 7.2).[18] At the very least, this means the time when Paul himself was among the Philippian congregation and writing letters to them when he was away (*Phil.* 3.2). The Pastoral Epistles and other Scriptures alluded to by Polycarp were part of his spiritual heritage.[19] Polycarp does not draw upon Titus, but it is highly unlikely that Polycarp knew nothing of Titus.

---

16. Laird ("Early Titles of the Pauline Letters") uniquely examines the titles given to the letters of Paul in the extant Greek collections of those writings. He determines on the basis of the uniformity of those titles that they were assigned at a very early stage in the development of the Pauline corpus. He argues that titles would only become necessary when multiple writings began to circulate as a collection. The purpose would be to distinguish these writings from each other. The evidence indicates that the Pauline corpus emerged early as the result of an editor or team of editors assembling the extant Pauline letters into a collection in preparation for circulation. Laird acknowledges the difficulty of tracing the early development of the Pauline corpus. It remains a matter of dispute when the earliest editions of the Pauline corpus emerged; however, Laird seems to feel that the extant second century collections of Paul's letters had their roots in the first century.

17. See Towner (*The Letters to Timothy and Titus*, 6), "It is highly unlikely that letters written at the turn of the century could, after just a decade or two or three, have been mistaken as coming from the Pauline mission."

18. Irenaeus, *Haer.* III.3.4. attests that Polycarp had first hand knowledge of the apostles who had seen Christ and received instruction from them. Irenaeus (130–202 CE) says that he was a youth when he saw the aged Polycarp.

19. See Berding, "Polycarp of Smyrna's View of the Authorship of 1 and 2 Timothy," 349–60. Berding points out that Polycarp arranges his allusions to Paul's writings around each of the three times he explicitly mentions the Apostle's name (in chapters 3, 9, and 11), and the first two times include allusions to 1 and 2 Timothy. This implies that Polycarp considers these texts Pauline.

Affirming the Author

Some scholars deny a first century provenance for the Pastoral Epistles because they were not included in the canon of Marcion of Sinope (c. 110–160), which he published in 140 CE However, Marcion also excluded the Gospels of Matthew, Mark, and John along with Hebrews, the General Epistles, the Johannine Epistles, Jude, and Revelation. He only included mutilated copies of twelve documents, Luke-Acts and ten of Paul's Epistles. His reasons for the shape of his canon were considered heretical. They were at least highly idiosyncratic and eccentric, and more specifically anti-Judaic and anti-Semitic. Marcion's exclusion of the Pastoral Epistles is more suspect than substantial.[20] Any arguments against the first century authorship of the Pastoral Epistles based on Marcion are well countered by reference to Clement and Polycarp.

Clement of Rome, Eusebius, and the Muratorian Canon mentions journeys of Paul after his first imprisonment in Rome.[21] This second wave of journeys, according to these narratives, end in a second imprisonment in Rome and execution. Clement says,

> Peter and Paul were the most notable examples of suffering under a tyrant emperor: There was Peter, who, because of unrighteous jealousy, endured not one or two but many trials, and thus having given his testimony went to his appointed place of glory. Because of jealousy and strife Paul by his example pointed out the way to the prize for patient endurance. After he had been seven times in chains, had been driven into exile, had been stoned, and had preached in the East and the West, he won the genuine glory for his faith, having taught righteousness to the whole world and having reached the farthest limits of the West. Finally, when he had given his testimony before the rulers, he thus departed from the world and went to the holy place, having become an outstanding example of patient endurance. (1 Clem 5.4–7)[22]

Peter and Paul were martyred between 64–68 CE. This phase leading to Paul's second Roman imprisonment and death seem to

---

20. See Towner, *Letters to Timothy and Titus*, 5.
21. 1 Clem 5:5–7; Eusebius, *Hist. eccl.* 2.22.7–8; *Mur. ca.* 38–39.
22. Holmes, *The Apostolic Fathers*, 35.

be the background for the Pastoral Epistles. Of course, many scholars view these texts and history with strigent skepticism. The debate at times becomes acrimonious. In the end, the skepticism only provides opportunity to sharpen the view of a more positive argument. All things considered, the case for the Pauline authorship of the Pastoral Epistles can be attacked, but it cannot be overturned.

7

Waiting for Vindication

The Bible and African American Women

A REGRETTABLE LEGACY

First Timothy 2:11–15 is one New Testament passage used to keep women "in their place" in both church and society. As I have tried to demonstrate in this study, this usage is uncalled for in the passage itself. This way of deploying the passage is entirely contrary to its meaning and message. The reception history of this passage will show numerous attempts by scholars to demonstrate incompatibility between the meaning of the text and the regrettable ways it has been used. However, these attempts have not been able to overcome all the interpretive difficulties of the text, particularly the statement that women shall be saved through childbearing. In some cases, the attempts have added more difficulty to interpreting the text. For these reasons, 1 Tim 2:11–15 has continued to be "oppressive," an "irredeemable text" or even a "text of terror" for many readers of the New Testament.[1] Many see the text *only* as a tool for delimiting opportunity or denying it all together for women who recognize a call

---

1. See Jacobs, "On 1 Timothy 2:9–15," 85–100; West, "Taming Texts of Terror," 160–73.

Women, Salvation, and Childbearing

to ministerial service or corporate leadership. By seeming to make spiritual salvation for women dependent upon their faithfulness to domestic responsibilities within the male-dominated household, the passage assigns a confined, restricted personhood to women. Childbearing literally understood is the chief responsibility of women in this regard. The irony is that this unique capability of women, which should be celebrated as nothing less than a miracle, is instead turned into a warrant for discrimination and repression. Instead of being celebrated for childbearing, women become penalized for childbearing, and moreover, defined by it to the exclusion of other abilities and skills. Moreover, the woman who has not borne or cannot bear children has, on the basis of this passage, been further dehumanized. She becomes marginalized within an already marginalized sector. If a woman's only claim to inclusion in the Kingdom of God is her ability to bear children, what becomes of the woman who has not, will not, or cannot exercise that function? She becomes demonized and implicitly assigned to cultural exile. At the same time a stream of conscious and unconscious biases from both men and women are evoked against her. She encounters barriers to every attempt she makes to live and be content.

African American women have especially suffered from discriminatory interpretations of Scripture, particularly passages like 1 Tim 2:11–15.[2] Like all women, the lives of African American women have been delimited and restricted on the basis of gender. Christian interpretations of 1 Timothy in both African American and White churches have reinforced this marginalization with emphases upon domestic roles and childbearing as the proper calling of women. However, racism has been a concurrent factor in the oppression of African American women. It has been another level of dehumanization. It is, however, hard to say which is the more immediate cause of dehumanization on a daily basis for Black women, racism or sexism. Black women experience both at the same time, all the time.

---

2. Weems, "Reading Her Way through the Struggle," 62–63. Weems observed, "Indeed, whether one considers their history from the context of North American women's history or African American history, one discovers that the Bible has been the most consistent and effective book that those in power have used to restrict and censure the behavior of African American women."

Waiting for Vindication

As long ago as 1973, sociologist Joyce A. Ladner said, "no other racial, ethnic, or religious group of females in the United States has undergone as much degradation, stereotyping, and actual punishment as Black women."[3] Sadly, her observation remains just as true today as it was decades ago.

Lisa L. Thompson describes how Black women's access to ordination, preaching, and the pulpit has been blocked by cultural preferences for maleness, whiteness, and a faith shaped by anti-blackness. In this context, she observes that "Black women remain some of the least regarded individuals in our world and still struggle for inclusion in both our social and religious conversations."[4]

Discriminatory forces want to restrict all women to the male-dominated household; but the Black household is already dominated by remote White racist institutional entities and the people who populate them. It is, in fact, not always correct to assume that there is a dominant Black male in the household in the first place. That is, if we use the term "dominant Black male" to indicate an adult male breadwinner. Black women are often left alone to battle a racist social-economic system.

According to the Institute of Women's Policy Research report on the *Status of Black Women in the United States*, about 80 percent of Black mothers support families as the sole breadwinner or as contributor of 40 percent of household income. Over sixty percent of Black women are in the workforce. A growing number of Black women own their own businesses at a rate exceeding all other racial ethnic groups of women and men; however, the unemployment rate for Black women was the highest among women from other racial ethnic groups.

The number of Black women who graduate with a bachelor's degree exceed that of Black men; however, the poverty rate for Black women is higher than that of Black men and women from other racial groups with the exception of Native American women. In recent times, Black women are more politically active than other

---

3. In her introduction to Staples, *The Black Woman in America*, x.
4. Thompson, *Ingenuity*, xii.

groups of men and women. Yet Black women are underrepresented in political offices at the state and federal level.

The median annual income for Black women is less than most women and men's income in the United States. Quality child care is unaffordable for most Black women with the average cost of care exceeding 20 percent of their median annual income.

The state and federal imprisonment rate for Black women is twice that of White women even though White women are a larger percentage of the population. A disproportionate number of Black girls are suspended from K–12 schools. The domestic violence rate for Black women is higher than that for White women. The mortality rate for Black women from heart disease, lung cancer, and AIDS is the highest among all racial ethnic groups.[5]

African American women comprise the highest percentage of front-line workers in essential services. Many of them hold jobs that cannot be done through telecommuting. Moreover, many depend upon public transportation which little protection from exposure. A disproportionate number of African American women were greatly impacted economically, emotionally, mentally, and biomedically by the COVID-19 pandemic. At the same time, there is a tendency within the medical community to be dismissive of Black women's health and medical complaints. Black women frequently complain that doctors do not take them seriously, and they complain with justifiable reason.

African American women find themselves facing a two-headed monster, racial and gender discrimination. To be sure, there are Black women who break out of the restricted roles imposed upon them. However, that does not mean that racism and sexism has gone away. In every case, regardless of what has been achieved, we still have to ask, "what more would have been achieved if racism and sexism were not factors in this woman's life?"

And then there are the women who have not been able to break out of the restricted roles imposed upon them. It is not because they have not tried. It is because wave after wave of systemic hindrances, barriers, and injustices have washed away their hopes

---

5. DuMonthier et al., *The Status of Black Women*.

and opportunities. There are people standing in the shadows behind these discouraging circumstances. These are the people who could have approved a loan, forgiven a debt, provided a job opportunity, paid what was owed, patronized a business, lent a helping hand, rendered a free service, shown compassion, demonstrated integrity, stood up for justice, or otherwise made a difference. White people do helpful things like these for each other all the time. But some will not do any of these things for a Black woman simply because she is black and a woman. We therefore still have to ask, "What more would have been achieved if racism and sexism were not factors in these women's lives?"

The pressing question for us is, How has Scripture interpretation contributed to the way women have been treated in society? This question, of course, drives my interest in a passage like 1 Tim 2:11–15, and particularly in how we should interpret the statement, "she shall be saved through childbearing." There is plenty of evidence that chauvinistic, patriarchal, and sexist interpretations of this passage have contributed to social injustices against women. This is especially clear when we realize how pervasive scripturally formed attitudes are in society. The real problem, of course, is that many of these scripturally formed attitudes are wrong attitudes formed by wrong interpretations of Scripture, not the Scripture alone. African American women are especially impacted. As Clarice Martin observes, "Black women are no strangers to arguments that the Bible sanctions their submission as wives and women in the domestic and socio-political spheres."[6]

We need to be clear. There is nothing wrong with occupying the household domestic role, neither for women nor men. Many women and men find great fulfillment in the roles performed within the bounds of the household: wife, husband, mother, father, child bearer, child-raiser, caretaker, nurturer, and provider. Many women and men are content to dedicate their lives to those roles and they should be affirmed and celebrated for doing so.

It is nevertheless wrong to restrict people to certain roles in society on the basis of race and gender, and even more so wrong to

---

6. Martin, "The *Haustafeln*," 222.

do this against their will. It is also wrong for society to deny people the resources they need to flourish and thrive in life, especially when this denial is on the basis of race and gender.

The problem is that many African American women are restricted to certain roles in life simply because they are black and women. They are denied opportunities for roles they want simply because they are black and women. One of the ways such discrimination and injustice manifests itself is through discriminatory interpretation of Scripture like 1 Tim 2:11–15.

Scripture can be an instrument of liberation or a tool of oppression. Regrettably, the reception history of 1 Tim 2:11–15 has too often shown how Scripture can be the latter. For this reason, I join others who have critiqued this history while at the same time offering insights into this passage that have never before been considered. However, I think that my insights are among the most radical ever offered. As I have pointed out, Augustine came closer than anyone to the thesis I argue. I discovered this feature of Augustine's thought only after formulating my own argument, and while investigating a history of interpretation upon the recommendation of a reviewer. However, Augustine's imposition of an allegorical reading upon the text of 1 Timothy was an otherwise ahistorical dogmatic choice. It is therefore not quite correct to call my approach "Augustinian." Nevertheless, despite Augustine's arbitrary allegorical dogmatism I was happy to find a historical figure leaning toward my argument.

My pivotal point is that *both women and men* are saved through childbearing, if we understand *childbearing* as the soul giving birth to virtues, particularly, the virtues faith, love, holiness, and temperance. These *virtues* are the *children* implied in 1 Tim 2:15. This is the very message of 1 Tim 2:11–15 using a theme drawn from its historical, cultural, and literary background. While strange to us, this would have been readily perceived by Paul's first century audience. As I pointed out, in the salvation-speech of the Pastoral Epistles, the birthing of virtues is subsequent to realized salvation, but prerequisite to eschatological salvation. African American women, and for that matter, all women, are therefore released from the idea that their worth and salvation are somehow dependent upon fulfilling narrowly defined domestic responsibilities centered on bearing children in the literal sense.

SLAVERY IN THE NEW TESTAMENT

Although my discussion of Scripture interpretation and African American women is based upon exegesis of 1 Tim 2:11–15 an additional exegetical component is required. We must also address the issue of slavery in the New Testament.[7] This is because instructions concerning women and slaves are part of the same table of ethics in 1 Timothy.[8] It is also because current racial discourse and attitudes in the United States continues to be shaped by past interpretations of "slavery texts" from the pre-Civil War era.[9] We therefore cannot ignore the biblical statement:

> Let all who are under the yoke of slavery count their own masters worthy of all honor lest the name and teaching of God be blasphemed. And let those who have believing masters not disrespect them, but because they are brothers, let them all the more serve them, those who are helped by their good service, because they are believers and beloved. These things teach and encourage. (1 Tim 6:1–2)

---

7. See the discussion of slavery in New Testament times in Martin, "Womanist Interpretation," 47. Martin says, "First, that slavery was an integral part of the social fabric of Paul's day is not in dispute, but the thesis that it was not a 'severe and cruel institution' has been challenged in recent years."

8. See Martin, "Somebody done hoodoo'd the hoodoo man," 216–17. Martin shows how White males of the Old South used the NT domestic codes to justify subordination of all women and Black people.

9. Cannon, "Ideology and Biblical Interpretation," 125–26. Cannon remarked, "Needless to say, the New Testament instructions that slaves should be obedient to their masters was interpreted as unqualified support for the modern institution of chattel slavery. The slave system was simply a part of the cosmos." On this and other myths, Cannon (127) further said, "I believe that it is important for us to trace the origin and expansion of these myths because the same general schemes of oppression and patterns of enslavement remain prevalent today and because the biblical hermeneutics of oppressive praxis is far from being dead among contemporary exegetes."

These instructions occur as part of the domestic codes or *Haustafeln* in New Testament epistolary literature (cf. Aristotle, *Pol.* 1.12). Similar instructions concerning slaves also appear in Titus 2:9-10; Eph 6:5-9; and Col 3:22—4:1, which are all from disputed letters of Paul.[10] We have different contexts for instructions in 1 Cor 7:21-24 and Phlm 8-21 which are undisputed letters of Paul. We also have instruction in 1 Pet 2:18 which is also part of a domestic code. In 1 Tim 6:1-2 we have a reluctant and forced acceptance of slavery, but only in the context of the Christian household. The author encourages Christian slaves to submit to masters so the Jesus movement does not draw negative attention. Such attention would be dangerous to the movement in the Roman Empire. Undermining the institution of slavery to any degree would be considered seditious activity in the Empire, and that would provoke violent military persecution of the church. Note that the author of 1 Timothy only addresses *Christian* slaves. They are the ones who hold the reputation of the Jesus movement in their hands. There is no general approval or support of slavery anywhere in the New Testament. It is only the reputation and safety of the Jesus movement that is at stake in these instructions. In Titus, Ephesians, and Colossians we see this same substratum of concern for the reputation and safety of the church. This is not support for slavery, this is concern for survival. In 1 Tim 6:2; Titus 2:9; Eph 6:9; Col 4:1, slave masters are also mentioned or instructed. As incongruent or contradictory as it may sound to us, we must remember that these are *Christian* slave masters that are being addressed. They are heads of Christian households. They are in fact being instructed to treat their slaves with justice and fairness. The combination of these instructions for slaves on the one hand, and slave masters on the other would transform the institution of slavery in the Christian household until it was no longer recognizable as slavery. We therefore see a consistency in the disputed Pauline Letters regarding slavery. In 1 Pet 2:18, only slaves are addressed, and again, they are Christians. Their masters may or may not be kind and gentle. They may even be abusive. In that case, the Petrine author encourages slaves to endure

---

10. Martin, "The *Haustafeln*," 213-25.

suffering, even if they are suffering unjustly. Again, the chief concern is to avoid undue attention in order to preserve the reputation and safety of the church (1 Pet 2:12).

These instructions in the New Testament letters indicate growing tensions between Christian identity and slavery in the Roman Empire. This means that there were growing tensions between Christians who were slaves and Christians who were slave masters. There would be no need for these instructions if these tensions did not exist. Whether or not the authors of these letters were Paul and Peter, there is recognition that many Christians may lose their lives and the church destroyed through military action if these tensions were not checked. In any case, there was never anything like approval or support for slavery in the New Testament; only a tense tolerance for the evil forced by threat of the Roman sword.

Regardless of where one stands on the authorship of 1 Timothy, it is telling that the author places "slave traders" (ἀνδραποδισταῖς, *andrapodistais*) in the same company with "lawless, ungodly, sinners, unholy, murderers, liars, the sexually immoral, and other deplorables (1:9–11).[11] The author could not hold back his real attitude toward slavery even while trying not to provoke a charge of sedition.[12]

In 1 Cor 7:21–24, Paul encourages Christian slaves to avail themselves of freedom whenever they see the opportunity. Moreover, if they were free when they became Christian, they should continue in that freedom. "You were bought with a price; do not become slaves of men" (7:23). Paul is being careful here. His exhortation that a Christian should "remain in the same state in which he was called" is designed to avoid citing a rebellion. It is clear that Paul hates slavery. He sees slavery as part of the demonic world order that will soon pass away (1 Cor 7:29–31; 15:24–27). Even

11. Martin ("1–2 Timothy and Titus," 419), who thinks that the Pastoral Epistles are pseudonymous, makes this observation about *andrapodistas*, "But what the term still strikingly represents, in any case, is biting anti-slavery polemic that requires further comment."

12. See Andria, "1 Timothy, 2 Timothy, Titus," 1475, "Paul does not support slavery—in fact he vigorously condemns the slave trade (1:10)—but he calls on slaves to live out what they believe and express it in respect for others."

when Paul speaks metaphorically, he shows his disdain for slavery (Gal 5:1).[13]

In his letter to Philemon, we see a close and personal engagement with a Christian slave master where Paul fully reveals his real attitude toward slavery. Again, Paul is careful not to break Roman law, so he determines to send Onesimus, the itinerant slave, back to Philemon, but as "no longer a slave, but more than a slave, as a beloved brother" (Phlm 16).

We therefore see a consistency between the disputed and undisputed letters of Paul on the subject of slavery. There is an underlying altogether rejection of slavery, but it is not made public for fear of Roman retaliation against the church. Instead, there is an attempt to transform the institution from within until it vanishes (1 Cor 12:13; Gal 3:28; Col 3:11).

Paul lived about nine decades after the Third Servile War (73–71 BCE), a conflict between Rome and rebel slaves led by Spartacus, a former gladiator from Thrace. After two years that rebellion was finally crushed by the Roman general Crassus and the eight legions he commanded. Ironically, Spartacus had an army of about 70,000, but was yet defeated (Plutarch, *Crass.* 8–11; Appian, *Hist. rom.* 1.539–60).

Paul had no army at all, let alone an army large and powerful enough to stand up against and defeat the Roman legions. If he had such an army, we could be sure that he would have done away with the Roman institution of slavery. As it stood, Paul's only option was to vanquish slavery by transforming it from within; by converting both slaves and slave masters to faith in Jesus Christ. This was also, the strategy of the author of 1 Timothy, whether that author was Paul or not.

When we cast our view wider, we must include Rev 18:1–13 where we have an implied condemnation of Rome for their trade in

---

13. See Patterson, "Paul, Slavery, and Freedom," 269. Patterson comments, "And here the evidence points overwhelmingly to the fact that Paul was a humane, caring soul in regard to slaves and their plight. Like many humane persons of his day, he clearly considered the condition of slavery a great misfortune and a personal tragedy. And we may reasonably surmise that he was strongly sympathetic to the provision of all legal means for the manumission of slaves."

"slaves, that is, human souls." Even in this case, the Revelator uses "Babylon" as a code name for Rome to protect his fellow Christians from possible reprisals. The whole New Testament including the disputed and undisputed Pauline Letters is consistent in its condemnatory attitude toward slavery.

The author of 1 Timothy therefore believes that slavery is evil, that women and men are equal, and that women and men are saved through the same gracious means. Contrary to the way 1 Timothy has been interpreted, there is a message of healing affirmation for those like African American women who must fight on the battlegrounds of both race and gender. It is especially when we get to the world behind these texts that we realize how wrong and misleading were attempts in the Antebellum American South to use Scripture to justify American chattel slavery.[14] In the original perspective beneath these texts, slavery is condemned and rejected. Pro-slavery Antebellum preachers and teachers were not revealing the heart of Scripture, but fleeing from it. They distorted the surface of Scripture to serve their heinous purposes. It is important for African American women and men to know this about the past because it also reveals the true character of the legacy we have inherited in the present. The racist and sexist messages that are communicated to us today in both overt and covert ways continue to be based upon distorted surface readings of the Scripture.

PHILO, PAUL, AND SLAVERY

Philo of Alexandria provides somewhat of a corroborating perspective on slavery in the world of Paul. The messages of Philo and Paul are clearly different, and there is no indication that the one is ever aware of the other; yet there are points where they converge. Philo criticizes those who are unable to think of slavery and freedom at the metaphorical level (*Prob.* 10). He distinguishes between slavery of the body and slavery of the soul, and makes a parallel distinction

---

14. See Martin, "Somebody done hoodoo'd the hoodoo man," 214–16, 218–19. Martin gives us a roster of pro-slavery advocates from pre-Civil War times.

between freedom of the body and freedom of the soul (*Prob.* 16–18). He exposes a paradox—the virtuous person is free, even though their bodies may be in bondage, and the vicious person is enslaved, even though they may possess wealth, power, and influence (*Prob.* 8–10, 20–21). Philo illustrates his point with a saying of Sophocles, "God is my ruler, and no mortal" (Θεὸς ἐμὸς ἄρχων, θνητὸς δ' οὐδείς, *Theos emos archōn thnētos d' oudeis*) (*Prob.* 19). Paul also speaks of slavery and freedom in a metaphorical sense (Rom 6:14–23; Gal 3:28; 4:1–11, 21–31; 5:1–15). This type of discourse was conventional in the literary world of Paul and Philo.

Despite his metaphorical applications, there are literal references to slavery in Philo's thought, just as there are in Paul's thought, and they are thoroughly negative. As Philo observes, "No one wants to be a slave" (*Prob.* 36) and "No slave is truly happy. For what greater affliction is there than to have no power over anything including oneself?" (*Prob.* 41). Philo is uncompromising in this judgment that death is preferable to slavery. He tells the story of the Laconian boy who chose death over slavery (*Prob.* 114). He praises the Dardanian women for drowning their own children rather than allowing them to be enslaved to the Macedonians (*Prob.* 115). He cites a script by Euripedes where the character Polyxena prefers death over slavery (*Prob.* 116). Philo maintains that whole populations of people, such as the Xanthians, were willing to fight to the death instead of being enslaved by the Romans (*Prob.* 118–120). Philo is not as reserved as Paul in his critique of slavery. It may be because Judaism's place in the Roman Empire was more secure than that of early Christianity. If so, then time will show that this place was falsely secure. In any case, Philo reveals that hatred of slavery was widespread in the ancient world. As he says:

> And this doctrine that freedom is glorious and honorable, slavery execrable and disgraceful, is attested by cities and nations, which are more ancient, more permanent, and, as far as mortals may be, immortal, and for immortals it is a law of their being that their every word is true. (*Prob.* 137)[15]

---

15. Colson, *Philo*, 89.

Indications are that Paul the Apostle shared in this hatred of slavery. Debates over Pauline authorship may continue, but regardless of where one comes out on the issue, the indications are that the author of 1 Timothy shared in this hatred of slavery.

TURNING A CORNER

Some may think it strange to address the social ramifications of Scripture interpretation. However, we have turned a corner in the academic study of Scripture. We have turned from the pretense of a detached, value-neutral, supposedly objective, supposedly universal, non-biased engagement with Scripture to a stance that recognizes a hidden reality in biblical exegesis. We all interpret Scripture from the standpoint of a cultural legacy.[16] We are either reinforcing a patriarchal, racist, sexist worldview and status quo, or we are dismantling it. This is because the detached, value-neutral, supposedly objective, supposedly universal, non-biased approach we have been pretending to have is really the patriarchal, racist, sexist worldview that has been the problem all along.

We in the field of biblical studies must now answer the question, how does my exegesis address the social ills and injustices that are wounding our world today? Gone are the days of ivory tower rhetoric and elitist discourse. We must now show "why does this argument matter at the level of the street?"

I have chosen to address the plight of African American women.[17] Since I have written on 1 Tim 2:11–15 which relates to women, salvation, and childbearing, I think it is clear why I should take up this particular discussion. I do not claim any special qualification to speak on the experiences of African American women. I am speaking instead on how Scripture interpretation has contributed to the

---

16. Cf. Tolbert, "Defining the Problem," 117. Tolbert says, "All interpretations are 'subjective,' that is, all readings are influenced by the vested interests and concerns of the interpreter."

17. In 2019, there were 48,221,39 African Americans in the United States. That was 14.7 percent of the American population (328.2 million). At 52 percent of the African American population, there were 23.5 million Black women.

oppression of African American women. I am especially concerned with the interpretation of 1 Tim 2:11–15. On historical and literary grounds, I maintain that the author of 1 Timothy himself intended that "childbearing" be understood metaphorically as part of an allegorical interpretation of Genesis 3. Although I am reluctant to say so myself, that is more radical than anything I have read.

Although I do not pretend to be one hundred percent objective and bias free in my interpretation of 1 Tim 2:11–15, I believe that I have advanced an interpretation of 1 Tim 2:11–15 that is both logically coherent and grounded in both literary and historical evidence. I have still made my best effort at eliminating bias and subjectivity in my argument. I think I have done as well as anyone.

Within the period of writing this chapter, a politically seismic event occurred in America. Senator Kamala D. Harris of California, an American of African and East Indian descent, has become the first woman elected Vice-President of the United States.[18] This was an historic occasion that will certainly have ramifications for the issues raised in this chapter. However, we are not able to declare that the issues are no longer relevant. Neither can we say that the barriers faced by African American women have disappeared. Clearly, the struggles continue, but they are now propelled by a historic victory.

18. On Saturday, November 7, 2020, major news outlets determined that enough votes had been counted in an extended count cycle to declare Kamala Harris Vice President-elect of the United States.

8

Expecting Better
Responding to Critics

A FALL FROM FAIRNESS

Criticisms of my "virtues as children" argument have been both interesting and disappointing—interesting because of their evasiveness, and disappointing for the same reason. One critic accused me of trying to "rescue Paul."[1] It is as if those who disparage Paul and Pauline thought have unquestionable claim to higher objectivity and a bias-free agenda. To maintain that Paul is chauvinistic and misogynistic seems to be sound doctrine to them, but to suggest that Paul is fair, equitable, and just is automatically suspect. For these critics, those who characterize Paul in a negative way are objective scholars, but those who characterize Paul in a positive way are somehow trying to "save" or "rescue" him. It has also been suggested that I am trying to make the text of Paul say what I heartily wish it would say as opposed to what it really says.[2] I imagine that those who make this suggestion have managed to avoid this pitfall in their own investigations, or at least they think they have. For the

---

1. Streete, "Response," 53.
2. Streete, "Response," 53.

record, these accusations, aside from being hypocritical claims, are simply not true. My aim is to understand and interpret Paul within his own social, cultural, literary, and historical context. I have found features of that context that have direct bearing on how we should read 1 Tim 2:11–15. I describe those features as "the virtues as children" theme. I also present the evidence that proves the theme. It would be better for critics to deal with the evidence rather than make guesses about my motives.

A number of criticisms that I find online make me wonder if the critic has actually taken the time to read my work. Many of these are so far off the mark that it is not worth the time to respond to them. Remarkably, a frequent type of response I have received to my work both online and in hard print is something I call the "one sentence dismissal."[3] It is most disheartening to experience this as a frequent response of professional scholars. Their responses give the clear impression that my work is cited only because it cannot be ignored, but at the same time the investigators do not want to deal with it. Therefore, they find a way to dismiss the work in one or two (maybe, three) sentences and then move on without any real engagement with my argument. Regarding 1 Tim 2:15, one critic seems to question whether my aim, along with others, is "to elucidate the phrase or to explain it away."[4] Since she offered no engagement with my argument her question is puzzling. I would expect someone who disagrees with my interpretation of 1 Tim 2:11–15 to at least show why she or he disagrees with my interpretation. I furthermore expect critics to deploy the normal procedure of demonstrating that my argument is (1) logically incoherent, (2) factually wrong, (3) missing important information, or (4) any combination of all of the above, that is, if they find my argument lacking in some way.

Instead, my rather detailed arguments are dismissed in one or two (maybe, three) sentences. The character of these dismissals

---

3. See Solevag, "Salvation, Gender, and the Figure of Eve," 2; Wessels, "Changing the Feminine Face of Poverty," 116n23, where my name is misspelled; Miller, "Saved through Childbearing?," 218n15; Zehr, *1&2 Timothy, Titus*, 68.

4. Solevag, "Salvation, Gender, and the Figure of Eve," 2.

is consistent. They either misrepresent what I have written, or they ignore what I have written. After reading so many of these one-sentence dismissals, I have come to the conclusion that they present no attempt to engage my argument because they cannot disprove my argument.

To be clear, I am open to the possibility that my proposal is no solution, and that I only think I have solved the problem when I have not really solved it. If that is the case, then someone ought to be able to show that I have not really solved it. Instead, some scholars choose to sidestep the work, and pretend like it is not there.

A NOTABLE EXCEPTION

I now want to acknowledge one notable exception to all that I have just said. In 2013, a *Scriptura* article was published by Elna Mouton of Stellenbosch University and Ellen van Wolde of Radboud University of Nijmegen entitled, "New Life from a Pastoral Text of Terror? Gender Perspectives on God and Humanity in 1 Timothy 2."[5] In this article Mouton and van Wolde point out that the author of 1 Timothy made selective use of elements from Genesis 2–3 and that this selectiveness may have jeopardized the transformative power of the text in "unthinkable ways" for "later audiences." This, they argue, challenges us to find ways to respect the text as "a product of its own time," yet allow it to speak in transformative ways to us in our own time.[6] They explore both literal and allegorical interpretations of 1 Tim 2:13–15 in response to this challenge.

Mouton and van Wolde astutely describe the notorious difficulty of 1 Tim 2:8–15 for New Testament scholarship and the church.

> For many people, 1 Timothy 2:8–15 is a canonical text that resists being read liberatively. It has probably become—especially since the nineteenth century—one of the most controversial texts from within the history of biblical interpretation relating to the participation

5. Mouton and van Wolde, "New Life," 583–601.
6. Mouton and van Wolde, "New Life," 596.

of women in church leadership and decision-making processes.⁷

They summon readers of 1 Timothy to find a new hermeneutic for the text *"so that the integrity of God's justice-seeking new creation will likewise be recognized by all."*⁸

In their exploration of options, Mouton and van Wolde call attention to my study:

> In contrast to the predominantly literal interpretation of 1 Timothy 2:11–15 that prevailed for a long time, a dramatically different perspective was presented by Kenneth L. Waters in an essay in *Journal of Biblical Literature* in 2004. Rather than reading it literally, Waters argued (2004: 703–704) that the "mode of cognition" of 1 Timothy 2:11–15 is that of an allegory.⁹

They follow with a detailed engagement with my argument for two more pages.¹⁰ This level of engagement with my article was a rare occurrence indeed, and continues to be. To this day, no other scholars have come close to this level of engagement with my article.

Mouton and van Wolde feel that my reading of 1 Tim 2:11–15 opens up new possibilities for the audience of 1 Timothy, but they warn that this allegorical reading may not be recognizable in the "(patriarchal) present." If this becomes the case, my allegorical reading may only endorse "a hierarchical interpretation of the creation story similar to that of a literal reading." They warn that there is no guarantee that my allegorical rhetoric "would have produced a counter-cultural interpretation of Genesis 2–3."¹¹

At this point, I must admit to difficulty understanding Mouton and van Wolde's warnings, or at least understanding what they seem to presuppose here. But I will try to engage. It seems that they are conflating 1 Timothy's twenty-first-century readership (us) with

---

7. Mouton and van Wolde, "New Life," 583.
8. Mouton and van Wolde, "New Life," 596.
9. Mouton and van Wolde, "New Life," 594.
10. Mouton and van Wolde, "New Life," 594–96.
11. Mouton and van Wolde, "New Life," 596.

the letter's first-century audience.[12] That would be a problem. The original first-century audience of 1 Timothy would not have had any difficulty understanding 1 Tim 2:11–15 allegorically. The first-century audience would not need to overcome a "hierarchical interpretation" of Genesis 2–3 because such an interpretation did not exist for them. The first-century audience would have immediately recognized "childbearing" in the letter to Timothy as a metaphor for "virtues-bearing." Clearly, twenty-first century readers of the letter must be instructed by scholars about the allegorical character of 1 Tim 2:11–15, but the letter's original first-century audience had no need of such instruction. They grew up on allegorical interpretation of ancient stories. Also, there is a difference between reading a text allegorically, and *recognizing* that a text *is* an allegory.[13] The Alexandrian school, for example, read texts allegorically even when they were *not* allegories. Philo and Augustine did the same. For us in the twenty-first century, it is not a matter of reading a text allegorically because we choose to, it is a matter of proving that a text *is* an allegory in its original intent and context. This is what I have tried to do in the case of 1 Tim 2:11–15. Mouton and van Wolde's final critique therefore misses my point about how 1 Tim 2:11–15 functions in its original context. Nevertheless, their study is a rare engagement with my work for which I am appreciative.[14]

I would not be concerned about the recognition of my work in the biblical studies guild if there was not so much at stake. Lives have been impacted in negative ways by racist and sexist framings of the biblical text. I think that I can contribute to the reversal of this situation. I therefore must rise to my own defense when scholars try to be dismissive of my work. I am not accusing critics of being racist or sexist because they are dismissive of my work, nor because they

---

12. Some scholars would insist upon a second century date for 1 Timothy, but that debate is beside the point that I am making here.

13. See Mouton and van Wolde, "New Life," 596n43. They suggest that if we read 1 Tim 2:11–15 allegorically, we might also read 6:1–2 allegorically. However, I think it is important to point out that, unlike 2:11–15, 1 Tim 6:1–2 is not an allegory. However, we can read 1 Tim 6:1–2 within the context of the early church's social and political dynamic as I have tried to do in this book.

14. I have thanked them personally in a private communication.

disagree with what I have written in this book or elsewhere. I am charging them with professional discourtesy when they deploy the "one sentence dismissal" as a substitute for actual engagement. I am sure that I am speaking for a multitude of other scholars whose careful work have been similarly dismissed.

APPENDIX

Exploring Further

Teknogonía in Classical Literature

The term τεκνογονία, *teknogonia* ("childbearing"), appears also in the writings of the physicians Hippocrates (460–377 BCE) and Galen (129–216 CE), and also in the works of the philosopher Aristotle (384–322 BCE) and anthologist Joannes Stobaeus (c. 455 CE). These sources are referenced by LSJ and BDAG but nevertheless hard to find and acquire.[1] I cite them more fully here.

Hippocrates, *Letters* 17, line 84, in Littré, *Hippocrates Opera Omnia* 9, 358:

> Ο δὲ, Ἡράκλεις, ἔφη, εἰς γὰρ δυνήσῃ με ἐλέγξαι, θεραπείην θεραπεύσεις... Καὶ πῶς οὐκ ἐλεγχθείης, ἐφην ὦ ἄριστε; ἤ οὐχ οἴῃ αἰτοπός γε εἶναι γελῶν ἀνθρώπου θάνατον ἤ νοῦσον ἤ ἤ παρακοπὴν... ἤ τοὔμπαλιν γάμους ἤ παηγύριας ἤ τεκνογονίην ἤ μυστήρια ἤ ἀρχὰς..., *O de Hrakleis, ephē, eis gar dynēsē me elegxai, therapeiēn therapeuseis... Kaipōs ouk elegchtheiēs, ephēn ō airiste; ē ouch oiē aitopos ge einai gelōn anthrōpou thanaton hē nouson hē hē parakopē... hē toumpalin gamous hē paēgyrias hē teknogoniēn hē mystēria hē archas.*

---

1. One other source, *CMG*, V. 9, 1 p. 27 1908, was inaccessible to me.

Exploring Further

And Hercules said, "Unless you refute me, you will heal me with a cure. . . ." and I said, "How can I refute you, O noble one, and not be out of place like a man laughing at death, disease, or delirium . . . or marriage, celebration, childbearing, mystery, or age."

Aristotle, *Historia Animalium* IX (VII) 582a28 in Balme, *Aristotle*, 475–76:

> μετὰ δὲ τὰ τρὶς ἑπτὰ ἔτη αἱ μέν γυναῖκες πρὸς τὰς τεκνογονίας ἤδη εὐκαίρως ἔχουσιν, οἱ δ' ἄνδρες ἔτι ἔχουσιν ἐπίδοσιν, *meta de ta tris epta etē ai men gynaikes pros tas teknogoniasēdē eukairōs echousin, hoi d' andres eti echousin epidosin*

> But with the twenty-first year women already have opportunity for childbearing and men still have something to give.

Stobaeus, *Ecl* II. 94.7 W. in Ab Arnim, *Stoicorum Veterum Fragmenta*, 158:

> καὶ τὸ νομοθετεῖν δὲ καὶ τὸ παιδεύειν ἀνθρώπους, ἔτι δὲ συγγράφειν τὰ δυνάμενα ὠφελεῖν τοὺς ἐντυγχάνοντας τοῖς γράμμασιν οἰκεῖον εἶναι τοῖς σπουδαίοις καὶ τὸ συγκαταβαίνειν καὶ εἰς γάμον καὶ εἰς τεκνογονίαν καὶ αὐτοῦ χάριν καὶ τῆς πατρίδος καὶ ὑπομένειν περὶ ταύτης ἐὰν ᾖ μετρία, καὶ πόνους καὶ θάνατου, *kai to nomothetein de kai to paideuein anthrōpous, eti de sungraphein ta dynamenaōphelein tous entynchanontas tois grammasin hoikeion einai tois spoudaiois kai to sunkatabainein kai eis gamon kai eis teknogonian kai autou charin kai tēs patridos kai hypomenein peri tautēs eanē metria kai ponous kai thanatou*

> The framing of laws, the disciplining of men, and the composition of things able to help those who pursue letters are proper for those who are dedicated, but, if one is moderate, surrendering to marriage, childbearing, and the blessing of family is to leave toil and death behind.

Exploring Further

Galeni In Hippocrates, 27:

ὑπὲρ ὧν ἔτι πλέον ἐν γε τῷ περὶ τεκνογονίας λόγῳ διερχόμεθα, *hyper ōn eti pleon en ge tō peri teknogonias logō dierchometha (CMG 112.48.10)*

Moreover, we shall obtain a comprehensive overview of childbearing in the present account.

Finally, ἡ τεκνογονία, *hē teknogonia,* is a feminine noun. The verbal form of the term is τεκνογονέω, *teknogoneō*. The noun form translates into English as a gerund, i.e., a verbal noun ("childbearing"). Notably, the term, *teknogonia* by itself does not automatically carry any specialized spiritual, metaphorical, nor mystical meaning as we see from the texts above. The term only means "childbearing." The metaphorical meaning of *teknogonia* that we discover in 1 Tim 2:15 is imposed upon the term by the author of the epistle; nevertheless, it is a meaning that the author draws from the literary, cultural, and historical environment of his audience. The author of 1 Timothy could have easily used the terms τίκτειν, τικτόμενος, or τεκνογονέω; *tiktein, tiktomenos,* or *teknogoneō* to the same effect.

Bibliography

Ab Arnim, Ioannes, ed. *Stoicorum Veterum Fragmenta*. Vol. 3. Stuttgart: Teubner, 1964.
Adlington, William, and S. Gaselee, trans. *The Golden Ass: Being the Metamorphoses of Lucius Apuleius*. Cambridge, MA: Harvard University Press, 1971.
Andria, Solomon. "1 Timothy, 2 Timothy, Titus." In *ABC*, 1469–86.
Apostle, Hippocrates G., trans. *Aristotle's Nicomachean Ethics*. Grinnell, IA: Peripatetic, 1984.
Arnold, C. E. "Ephesus." In *DPL*, 249–52.
Attridge, Harold W., et al. "The Tripartite Tractate (I, 5)." In *NHL*, 58–103.
August, Jared M. "What Must She Do To Be Saved? A Theological Analysis of 1 Timothy 2:15." *Them* 45 (2020) 84–97.
Balme, D. M., ed. *Aristotle: Historia Animalium I*. Cambridge: Cambridge University Press, 2002.
Bassler, Jouette M. *1 Timothy, 2 Timothy, Titus*. ANTC. Nashville: Abingdon, 1996.
Bauckham, Richard. *Gospel Women: Studies of the Named Women in the Gospels*. Grand Rapids: Eerdmans, 2002.
Berding, Kenneth. "Polycarp of Smyrna's View of the Authorship of 1 and 2 Timothy." *VC* 53 (1999) 349–60.
Bethge, Hans-Gebhard, and Bentley Layton, trans. "On the Origin of the World (II, 5 and XIII, 2)." In *NHL*, 170–89.
Betz, Hans Dieter. *Galatians: A Commentary on Paul's Letter to the Churches in Galatia*. Hermeneia. Philadelphia: Fortress, 1979.
Brooten, Bernadette. "Junia... Outstanding among the Apostles (Romans 16:7)." In *Women Priests: A Catholic Commentary on the Vatican Declaration*, edited by Leonard Swidler and Arlene Swidler, 141–44. New York: Paulist, 1977.
Burchard, C. trans. "Joseph and Aseneth." In *OTP*, 2:175–247.

BIBLIOGRAPHY

Burer, Michael. "ΕΠΙΣΗΜΟΙ ΕΝ ΤΟΙΣ ἈΠΟΣΤΟΛΟΙΣ in Rom 16:7 as 'Well Known to the Apostles': Further Defense and New Evidence." *JETS* 58 (2015) 731–55.

Burer, Michael, and Daniel Wallace. "Was Junia Really an Apostle? A Reexamination of Romans 16:7." *NTS* 47 (2001) 76–78.

Butler, Harold Edgeworth, trans. *The Institutio Oratoria of Quintilian*. 4 vols. Cambridge, MA: Harvard University Press, 1966.

Calvin, John, *Commentaries on the First Epistle to Timothy*. Translated by William Pringle. CC 21. Grand Rapids: Baker, 1993.

Campbell, Thomas L. *Dionysius the Pseudo-Areopagite: The Ecclesiastical Hierarchy*. Washington, DC: University Press of America, 1981.

Cannon, Katie Geneva. "Ideology and Biblical Interpretation." In *The Recovery of Black Presence: An Interdisciplinary Exploration*, edited by Randall C. Bailey and Jacquelyn Grant, 119–28. Nashville: Abingdon, 1995.

Capes, David B., et al. *Rediscovering Paul: An Introduction to His World, Letters, and Theology*. Downers Grove, IL: IVP, 2007.

Charlesworth, James H. trans. "Odes of Solomon." In *OTP*, 2:726–71.

Collins, Raymond F. *I &II Timothy and Titus: A Commentary*. NTL. Louisville: Westminster John Knox, 2002.

———. "The Theology of the Epistle to Titus." *ETL* 76 (2000) 56–72.

Colson, F. H. trans. *Philo: Every Good Man Is Free. On the Contemplative Life. On the Eternity of the World. Against Flaccus. Apology for the Jews. On Providence*. LCL 363. Cambridge, MA: Harvard University Press, 1941.

Colson, F. H., and G. H. Whitaker, trans. *Philo: On the Confusion of Tongues. On the Migration of Abraham. Who Is the Heir of Divine Things? On Mating with the Preliminary Studies*. LCL 261. Cambridge, MA: Harvard University Press, 1932.

Cooper, John M., and D. S. Hutchinson, eds. *Plato: Complete Works*. Indianapolis: Hackett, 1997.

Coupland, Simon. "Salvation through Childbearing? The Riddle of 1 Timothy 2:15." *ExpTimes* 112 (2001) 302–3.

Couser, Greg A. "God and Christian Existence in the Pastoral Epistles: Toward Theological Method and Meaning." *NovT* 42 (2000) 262–83.

Cross, F. I., and E. A. Livingstone. "Allegory." In *ODCC*, 37–38.

Davison, Richard M. *Typology in Scripture: A Study of Hermeneutical τύπος Structures*. AUSDDS 2. Berrien Springs, MI: Andrews University Press, 1981.

Dawson, David. *Allegorical Readers and Cultural Revision in Ancient Alexandria*. Los Angeles: University of California Press, 1992.

Dibelius, Martin, and Hans Conzelmann. *The Pastoral Epistles*. Hermeneia. Philadelphia: Fortress, 1972.

Donelson, Lewis R. *Colossians, Ephesians, 1 and 2 Timothy, and Titus*. Louisville: Westminster John Knox, 1996.

DuMonthier, Asha, et al. *The Status of Black Women in the United States*. Washington, DC: IWPR, 2017.

Bibliography

Dunn, James D. G. "The First and Second Letters to Timothy and the Letter to Titus." In *NIB*, edited by Leander C. Keck et al., 11:773-880. Nashville: Abingdon, 2000.

———. "Paul's Epistle to the Romans: An Analysis of Structure and Argument." In *ANRW* 25/4, edited by Wolfgang Haase, 2842-90. Berlin: de Gruyter, 1987.

Epp, Eldon Jay. *Junia: The First Woman Apostle*. Minneapolis: Fortress, 2005.

Evelyn-White, Hugh G., trans. *Hesiod: The Homeric Hymns. Epic Cycle. Homerica*. LCL 57. Cambridge, 2002.

Fee, Gordon D. *Gospel and Spirit: Issues in New Testament Hermeneutics*. Peabody, MA: Hendrickson, 1991.

Fitzmyer, Joseph. "The Structured Ministry of the Church in the Pastoral Epistles." *CBQ* 66 (2004) 582-96.

Fowler, Harold North, trans. *Plato: Euthyphro. Apology. Crito. Phaedo. Phaedrus*. LCL 36. Cambridge, MA: Harvard University Press, 1971.

Galeni In Hippocrates De Natura Homines in Corpus Medicorum Graecorum. Lipsiae et Berolini: Teubner, 1914.

García Martínez, Florentino, and Wilfred G. E. Watson, trans. *The Dead Sea Scrolls Translated: The Qumran Texts in English:* Grand Rapids: Eerdmans, 1996.

Gathercole, Simon. "The Justification of Wisdom (Matt 11:19b/Luke 7:35)." *NTS* 49 (2003) 476-88.

Gorday, Peter, ed. *Colossians, 1-2 Thessalonians, 1-2 Timothy, Titus, Philemon*. ACCS 9. Downers Grove, IL: IVP, 2000.

Gordon, T. David. "A Certain Kind of Letter: The Genre of 1 Timothy." In *Women in the Church: A Fresh Analysis of 1 Timothy 2:9-15*, edited by Andreas J. Köstenberger et al., 53-64. Grand Rapids: Baker, 1995.

Graves, Robert, trans. *The Transformation of Lucius, Otherwise Known as The Golden Ass*. New York: Farrar, Straus, and Giroux, 1979.

Grube, G. M. A. trans. *Pheado in Plato: Complete Works*. Edited John M. Cooper and D. S. Hutchinson. Indianapolis: Hackett, 1997.

Gupta, Nijay K. "Reconstructing Junia's Imprisonment: Examining a Neglected Pauline Comment in Romans 16:7." *PRS* 47 (2020) 385-97.

Hall, Jonathan M. "Ionians." In *EGHT*, edited by Graham Speake, 1:820-21. Chicago: Fitzroy Dearborn, 2000.

Hanson, J. Arthur, trans., *Apuleius Metamorphoses (The Golden Ass), Volume II: Books 7-11*. LCL 453. Cambridge, MA: Harvard University Press, 1989.

Harrington, D. J., trans. *Pseudo-Philo*. In OTP, 2:297-377.

Hays, Richard B. *Echoes of Scripture in the Letters of Paul*. New Haven: Yale University Press, 1989.

———. "The Letter to the Galatians: Introduction, Commentary, and Reflections." In *NIB*, edited by Leander E. Keck et al, 11:181-348. Nashville: Abingdon, 2000.

Hengel, Martin. *Judaism and Hellenism: Studies in Their Encounter in Palestine during the Early Hellenistic Period*. Eugene, OR: Wipf & Stock, 1974.

Bibliography

Hollander, Harm W., and Gijsbert E. van der Hout. "The Apostle Paul Calling Himself an Abortion: 1 Cor. 15:8 within the context of 1 Cor. 15:8–10." *NovT* 38 (1996) 224–36.

Holmes, Michael W., ed. *The Apostolic Fathers: Greek Texts and English Translations*. Grand Rapids: Baker, 1999.

Hurtado, Larry W. "The Gospel of Mark: Evolutionary or Revolutionary Document." *JSNT* 40 (1990) 15–32.

Huttar, David. "Did Paul Call Andronicus an Apostle in Romans 16:7?" *JETS* 52 (2009) 747–78.

Jacobs, Maretha M. "On 1 Timothy 2:9–15: Why Still Interpret 'Irredeemable' Biblical Texts?" *Scriptura* 88 (2005) 85–100.

Johnson, E. Elizabeth. "Romans 9–11: The Faithfulness and Impartiality of God." In *Pauline Theology III: Romans*, edited by David M. Hay and E. Elizabeth Johnson, 211–39. Minneapolis: Fortress, 1995.

Johnson, Lee A. "Paul's Letters Reheard: A Performance-Critical Examination of the Preparation, Transportation, and Delivery of Paul's Correspondence." *CBQ* 79 (2017) 60–76.

Johnson, Luke Timothy. *The First and Second Letter to Timothy*. AB 35A. New York: Doubleday, 2001.

Keener, Craig S. *Galatians: A Commentary*. Grand Rapids: Baker, 2019.

Kelly, J. N. D. *A Commentary on the Pastoral Epistles: Timothy I & II, Titus*. San Francisco: Harper & Row, 1987.

Kennedy, George, trans. *Progymnasmata: Greek Textbooks of Prose Composition and Rhetoric*. SBLWGRW 10. Atlanta: SBL, 2003.

Kroeger, Richard Clark, and Catherine Clark Kroeger. *I Suffer Not A Woman: Rethinking 1 Timothy 2:11–15 in Light of Ancient Evidence*. Grand Rapids: Baker, 1992.

Laird, Benjamin. "Early Titles of the Pauline Letters and the Formation of the Pauline Corpus." *BibNot* 175 (2017) 55–81.

Liefield, Walter. "Response to 1 Timothy 2:12: A Classicist View by Catherine Clark Kroeger." In *Women, Authority, and the Bible*, edited by Alvera Mickelsen, 244–48. Downers Grove, IL: IVP, 1986.

Lin, Yii-Jan. "Junia: An Apostle before Paul." *JBL* 139 (2020) 191–209.

Littré, Emilie, ed. *Hippocrates Opera Omnia 9*. Amsterdam: Hakkert, 1962.

Lodge, John G. *Romans 9–11: A Reader-Response Analysis*. USFISFCJ 6. Atlanta: Scholars, 1996.

Long, A. A. "The Scope of Early Greek Philosophy." In *CCEGP*, edited by A. A. Long, 1–21. Cambridge: Cambridge University Press, 1999.

Luther, Martin. *Lectures on Genesis Chapters 26–30*. Edited by Jaroslav Pelikan and Walter A. Hansen. Luther's Works 5. St. Louis: Concordia, 1968.

MacRae, G., trans. "Apocalypse of Adam." In *OTP*, 1:708–19.

Marcus, Ralph, trans. *Philo: Questions and Answers on Genesis*. LCL 380. Cambridge, MA: Harvard University Press, 1953.

Marshall, I. Howard, and Philip H. Towner. *A Critical and Exegetical Commentary on The Pastoral Epistles*. ICC. Edinburgh: T. & T. Clark, 1999.

Martin, Clarice J. "1–2 Timothy and Titus (the Pastoral Epistles)." In *TNL*, 409–36.

———. "The *Haustafeln* (Household Codes) in African American Biblical Interpretation: 'Free Slaves' and 'Subordinate Women.'" In *SRWT*, 206–31.

———. "'Somebody done hoodoo'd the hoodoo man': Language, Power, Resistance, and the Effective History of Pauline Texts in American Slavery." *Semeia* 83/84 (1998) 203–33.

———. "Womanist Interpretation of the New Testament: The Quest for Holistic and Inclusive Biblical Translation and Interpretation." *JFSR* 6 (1990) 41–61.

McDonald, L. M. "Ephesus." In *DNTB*, 318–21.

Meeks, Wayne A. *The First Urban Christians: The Social World of the Apostle Paul*. New Haven: Yale University Press, 1983.

Metzger, Bruce. *A Textual Commentary on the Greek New Testament*. Philadelphia: United Bible Societies, 1971.

Miller, Jeff. "Saved through Childbearing? 1 Timothy 2:15 as a Hermeneutical Caveat." *SCJ* 20 (2017) 215–25.

Mitchell, Matthew W. "Reexamining the 'Aborted Apostle': An Exploration of Paul's Self-Description in 1 Corinthians 15:8." *JSNT* 25 (2003) 469–85.

Mounce, William D. *The Pastoral Epistles*. WBC 46. Nashville: Thomas Nelson, 2000.

Mouton, Elna, and Ellen van Wolde. "New Life from a Pastoral Text of Terror? Gender Perspectives on God and Humanity in 1 Timothy 2." *Scriptura* 111 (2012/2013) 583–601.

Murphy-O'Connor, Jerome. "Interpolations in 1 Corinthians." *CBQ* 48 (1986) 81–94.

Odell-Scott, David W. "In Defense of an Egalitarian Interpretation of 1 Cor 14:34–36: A Reply to Murphy-O'Connor's Critique." *BTB* 17 (1987) 100–103.

———. "Let the Women Speak in Church: An Egalitarian Interpretation of 1 Cor 14:33b–36." *BTB* 13 (1983) 90–93

———. "The Paulinist Reversal of Paul's Critique of Gender Subordination: Ephesians 5 and 1 Corinthians 11." Paper presented at the SBL Annual Meeting, Boston, MA, November 22, 1999.

Orr, William F., and James Arthur Walther. *1 Corinthians: A New Translation, Introduction, with a Study of the Life of Paul, and Commentary*. AB 32. Garden City, NY: Doubleday, 1976.

Padgett, Alan. "Wealthy Women at Ephesus: 1 Timothy 2:8–15 in Social Context." *Interpretation* 41 (1987) 19–31.

Patterson, Orlando. "Paul, Slavery, and Freedom: Personal and Socio-Political Reflections." *Semeia* 83/84 (1998) 263–79.

Perriman, Andrew C. "What Eve Did, What Women Shouldn't Do: The Meaning of ΑΥΘΕΝΤΕΩ 1 Timothy 2:12." *TynBul* 44 (1993) 129–42.

Peters, F. E. *The Harvest of Hellenism*. New York: Simon and Schuster, 1970.

Philostratus, Flavius. *Heroikos*. Edited by Jennifer K. Berenson and Ellen Bradshaw Aitken. WGRW. Atlanta: SBL, 2001.

Porter, Stanley E. "What Does It Mean to be 'Saved by Childbirth' (1 Timothy 2:15)." *JSNT* 49 (1993) 87–102.

Prior, M. "Revisiting the Pastoral Epistles." *ScrB* 31 (2001) 2–19.

Quinn, Jerome D., and W. C. Wacker. *The First and Second Letters to Timothy*. Grand Rapids: Eerdmans, 2000.

Rackham, H., trans. *Aristotle: Nicomachean Ethics*. LCL 73. Cambridge, MA: Harvard University Press, 1926.

Räisänen, Heikki. *Paul and the Law*. Tübingen: Mohr Siebeck, 1993.

Ramelli, Ilaria L. E. "The Pastoral Epistles and Hellenistic Philosophy: 1 Timothy 5:1–2, Hierocles, and the 'Contraction of Circles.'" *CBQ* 73 (2011) 562–81.

Robinson, James M., ed, *The Nag Hammadi Library in English*. 3rd ed. New York: HarperCollins, 1988.

Robinson, William C., Jr., and Maddalena Scopello, trans. "The Exegesis of the Soul (II, 6)." In *NHL*, 190–98.

Rouse, W. H. D., trans. *The Complete Texts of Great Dialogues of Plato*. New York: Plume, 1961.

Rubinkiewicz, R., and H. G. Lunt. "Apocalypse of Abraham." In *OTP*, 1:681–705.

Ruether, Rosemary Radford. *Women and Redemption: A Theological History*. 2nd ed. Minneapolis: Fortress, 2012.

Sanders, E. P. *Paul and Palestinian Judaism: A Comparison of Patterns of Religion*. Philadelphia: Fortress, 1977.

Schaff, Philip, ed. *Augustin: On the Holy Trinity, Doctrinal Treatises, Moral Treatises*. NPNF 3. Peabody, MA: Hendrickson, 1995.

Schneemelcher, Wilhelm, and R. McL. Wilson, eds. *New Testament Apocrypha*. 2 vols. Louisville: Westminster John Knox, 1991–92.

Schofield, Malcolm. "The Ionians." In *From the Beginnings to Plato*, edited by C. C. W. Taylor. RHP 1. London: Routledge, 1997.

Scholer, David M. "1 Timothy 2:9–15 and the Place of Women in the Church's Ministry." In *Women, Authority, and the Bible*, edited by Alvera Mickelsen, 193–219. Downers Grove, IL: IVP, 1986.

Schreiner, Thomas R. "An Interpretation of 1 Timothy 2:9–15: A Dialogue with Scholarship." In *Women in the Church: A Fresh Analysis of 1 Timothy 2:9–15*, edited by Andreas J. Köstenberger et al., 150–51. Grand Rapids: Baker, 1995.

Schüssler Fiorenza, Elisabeth. *In Memory of Her: A Feminist Theological Reconstruction of Christian Origins*. New York: Crossroad, 1984.

Skalko, John J. "The Incoherence of Gender as a Social Construct." *EM* 45 (2020) 1–2.

Smyth, Herbert Weir. *Greek Grammar*. Cambridge, MA: Harvard University Press, 1976.

Solevag, Anna Rebecca. "Salvation, Gender, and the Figure of Eve in 1 Timothy 2:9–15." *LectioD* 2 (2012) 1–27.

BIBLIOGRAPHY

Standhartinger, Angela. "Colossians and the Pauline School." *NTS* 50 (2004) 572–93.
Staples, Robert. *The Black Woman in America: Sex, Marriage, and the Family*. Chicago: Nelson-Hall, 1979.
Streete, Gail P. C. "Response: Are Women Interested?" *LTQ* 42 (2007) 51–58.
Stuckenbruck, Loren T. "Why Should Women Cover Their Heads Because of Angels? (1 Corinthians 11:10)." *SCJ* 4 (2001) 205–34.
Thompson, Lisa L. *Ingenuity: Preaching as an Outsider*. Nashville: Abingdon, 2018.
Thurston, Bonnie Bowman. "The Theology of Titus." *HBT* 21 (1999)171–84.
Tolbert, Mary Ann. "Defining the Problem: The Bible and Feminist Hermeneutics." *Semeia* 28 (1983) 113–26.
Towner, Philip H. *The Letters to Timothy and Titus*. NICNT. Grand Rapids: Eerdmans, 2006.
———. "The Portrait of Paul and the Theology of 2 Timothy: The Closing Chapter of the Pauline Story." *HBT* 21 (1999) 151–70.
Vermes, Geza, trans. *The Complete Dead Sea Scrolls in English*. New York: Penguin, 1998.
Waterfield, Robin, trans. *The First Philosophers: The Presocratics and Sophists*. Oxford World's Classics. Oxford: Oxford University Press, 2000.
Waters, Kenneth L., Sr. "Empire and the Johannine Epistles." *RevExp* 114 (2017) 542–57.
———. *Mobile Ed: NT 225: Survey of the Pastoral Epistles*. Bellingham, WA: Lexham, 2015.
———. "Paul and Predestination: The Rhetoric of Impersonation in Romans 9:11–33." In *Afrocentric Interpretations of Paul and the Pauline Tradition: Things That Black Scholars See That White Scholars Do Not See*, edited by Thomas B. Slater, 39–97. Lewiston, NY: Mellen, 2018.
———. "Revisiting Virtues as Children: 1 Timothy 2:15 as Centerpiece for an Egalitarian Soteriology." *LTQ* 42 (2007) 37–49.
———. "Saved through Childbearing: Virtues as Children in 1 Timothy 2:11–15." *JBL* 123 (2004) 703–35.
Weems, Renita J. "Reading Her Way through the Struggle: African American Women and the Bible." In *SRWT*, 57–77.
Welch, P. G., trans. *Apuleius: The Golden Ass*. Oxford: Oxford University Press, 1995.
Wessels, Johannes M. "Changing the Feminine Face of Poverty—Reading 1 Timothy 2:15 from a Socio-economic Perspective." *Neot* 50 (2016) 105–22.
West, Gerald. *Taming Texts of Terror: Reading (Against) the Gender Grain of 1 Timothy*." *Scriptura* 86 (2004) 160–73.
Wisse, Frederik, trans. "The Paraphrase of Shem (VII, I)." In *NHL*, 339–61.
Wolters, Al. "ΙΟΥΝΙΑΝ (Romans 16:7) and the Hebrew Name Yĕḥunnī." *JBL* 127 (2008) 397–408.
Wright, N. T. *Paul and the Faithfulness of God*. COQG 4. Minneapolis: Fortress, 2013.

Bibliography

Wright, R. B., trans. "Psalms of Solomon." In *OTP*, 2:639–70.
Yonge, C. D. trans. *The Works of Philo*. Peabody, MA: Hendrickson, 1997.
Young, Frances Margaret. *The Theology of the Pastoral Letters*. NTT. Cambridge: Cambridge University Press, 1994.
Zehr, Paul M. *1&2 Timothy, Titus*. BCBC. Scotsdale, PA: Herald, 2010.

Subject-Name Index

Abelard, Peter, 60
Abraham, 7n15, 24, 75
Acts of Paul and Thecla, 13n33
Adam, 9-12, 15, 17, 24
Adam/Christ contrast, 17
Adlington, William, 39n18
Aeschylus, 38n14
African American population,103n17,
Agricultural reproductive metaphor, 7, 21, 28, 28n28, 51
Alexander, 80
Alexandria, 1,4n9, 38nn13-14
Allegorical interpretation, 2 n1, 10, 10n22, 22, 22n14, 38, 38n13, 50, 51, 78, 96,107, 109
Allegory, 3, 4, 78, 108, 109
Ambrosiaster, 48, 58, 60
Anaximander, 37n9
Anaximenes, 37n9
Anaxigoras, 37n9
Ancient letter writing, 82, 83, 84
Andria, Solomon, 55n5, 99n12
Androcentric culture,2
Andronicus, See Junia and Andronicus

Anencletus, bishop of Rome, 85
Angels, 69, 70, 71
Anthrōpos as "human" or "man," 8n17
Apodosis and protasis, 47, 50
Apollo, 39, 39n18
Apollos, co-worker of Paul, 56, 80
Apostle, Hippocrates G., 28n28
Apostle, meaning of, 57, 58, 61
Apphia, 55, 74
Apuleius, 39, 69
Aquila, see Prisca and Aquila
Archonic beings, 19, 25
Aratus, 29n32
Aristarchus, 58
Arnim, Ab, 112
Artemas, Greek fertility goddess, 39, 39n18, 40, 40n19, 41, 51
Artemas, male co-worker of Paul, 56, 80
Argos, 30n33
Arnold, C.E., 36n5
Aristotle, 28, 30, 98, 111
Arphaxad, 8 n16
Ascetic tendency, 13, 13n33, 14n41
Asclepius, 29n29
Attic dialect of Greek, 38n14

123

Subject-Name Index

Attridge, Harold W., 70n52
Augustine of Hippo, 49, 50, 96
August, Jared, 16, 17, 17nn47–50
Authorship, 79, 80, 82, 83
   Pauline, 79, 80, 90
   Pseudonymous, 80, 81, 83, 84
   Single (Pastoral Epistles), 9n19, 79n1
   Skepticism, 90
Autobiographical statements, 81
Azusa Pacific University, xxii

Balme, D.M., 112
Bassler, Jouette M., 4n6, 10n20, 11n25, 13n37
Bauckham, Richard, 61, 61n26
Berding, Kenneth, 88n19
Bethge, Hans-Gebhard, 18n1
Bethuel, 15n43
Betz, Hans Dieter, 65n40
Biblical tradition, 10
Biblical exegesis of Genesis, 25
Birth of *the child*, 16, 17
Birthing and abiding, 6
Bohairic Coptic version, 58
Brooten, Bernadette, 58, 58n8, 60, 61
Burchard, C, 33n45
Burer, Michael, 61, 61n26, 62, 62n29
Butler, Harold Edgeworth, 68n46

Callimachus, 39
Calvin, John, 49, 49n14
Campbell, Thomas L., 31n40
Cannon, Katie Geneva, 97n9
Capes, David, 82, 83, 83nn4–9
Carpus, 80
Cebes, 27
Cenchreae, 55, 69
Cerberus, 29n29
Charlesworth, James, 6n14
Chronology, 84, 88, 89
Chrysostom, 60

Childbearing, 3, 5, 7n15, 10n22, 13–15, 21, 25, 26, 35, 40, 41, 46, 48, 49, 50–52, 52n27, 54, 78, 96, 103, 104, 109, 111–13
Children of Abraham, 75
Children of Noah, 7, 22
Children of the soul, 2, 26, 26n21, 27
Child of Mary, 13
Chloe, 55, 74
Christians, Christianity, 81, 98, 99, 102
Christ, 21, 22, 30n33, 31, 34, 34n1, 35, 42–46, 48, 56, 57, 61, 63–66, 74–76, 100
Christological interpretation, 16
Circumcision, uncircumcision, 2n1, 75
Clark Kroeger, Richard and Catherine, 12, 12nn27–30, 12n32, 13, 13n33, 14, 39, 39n16, 52n27
Claudia, 64, 80
Cleanthes, 29n32
Clement of Alexandria, 4n9, 48
Clement of Rome, 84, 85, 85n10, 86, 87, 87n15, 88, 89
Clement, co-worker of Paul, 56, 86
Collins, Raymond F., 4n8, 11n25, 15n41, 45n17
Colossae, 55, 64, 74
Colson, F.H., 6n13, 24n16, 102n15
Commonplace, 18, 21, 37, 39, 39n15
Context-specific application, 9
Conzelmann, Hans, 14n41
Cooper, John M., ix
Corinth, 41n20, 55, 69, 70, 84
Coupland, Simon, 14, 14n40, 52n27
Couser, Greg A., 45n18
COVID-19 pandemic, 94
Crassus, 100
Creation order, 3, 4n6

Subject-Name Index

Crescens, 80
Crete, 80, 82
Cross, F.L., 5 n9

Damascene, John, 60
Davila, EJ, xxii
Davison, Richard M., 11n23
Dawson, David, 3 n2, 11n23
Dead Sea Scrolls, 32, 32nn41–42
Death (as a Gnostic archon), 18
Delegated letters, 83, 84
Demas, 80, 87
Democritus, 37n9
Deutero-Pauline, 14, 14n40
Diana, the goddess, 39
Dibelius, Martin, 14n41
Diotima of Mantineia, 26, 27, 41n20
Domitian, emperor of Rome, 85, 86
Donelson, Lewis R., 31n37, 43n3, 44n12
DuMonthier, Asha, 94n5
Dunn, James D.G., 10n20, 53n2

Egalitarian view of women, 54, 55n4, 64, 65, 71, 72, 78
Eileithyia, Eileithyiae, goddesses of childbirth, 30n33, 40n19, 41n20
Eluma, 21n10
Empedocles, 37n9
Epaphras, 55, 56, 58, 64
Epaphroditus, 56
Epimenides, 29n32
Ephesus, 3, 4, 9, 12, 36, 39, 40n19, 41, 51, 55, 80, 82
Ephesian congregation, 9, 11
Epp, Eldon Jay, 58, 58n8, 60, 61
Erastus, 80
Esau, 24
Eubulus, 80
Euripides, 38n14, 102
Eusebius, 85, 89
Euodia and Syntyche, 56, 64

Eurytheus, 30n34
Eve, 9, 10, 11, 12, 13, 15, 15n42, 17, 24, 25
Evidence, literary and historical, 3

Faith, various senses of, 44
False teachers, 11, 13
Farmer, William, xxii
Father, the, 26
Fee, Gordon D., 10n22, 11n26
Female imagery in Galatians, 75, 76, 77
Figurative interpretation, 3, 4, 10n22
First-century audience of Paul, 109
First declension masculine nouns, 59
First and second imprisonment of Paul, 89
Fitzmyer, Joseph, 79n1
Four cardinal virtues, 5n11
Four cardinal vices, 30n36
Fowler, Harold North, 28n24
Freedom, 76, 101, 102
Fruit bearing, 6, 7n15, 21, 26, 28, 34
Fruit of the soul, 7n15
Fruit of the womb, 7n15
Fuller Theological Seminary, xxii

Galen, 111
García Martínez, Florentino, 32nn42–44
Gaselee, S. 39n18
Gathercole, Simon, 34n1
Gender-inclusive terms, 46
Generative concept of virtue, 28
Geneva Scholium on *Illiad* XXI, the, 38n11
Gentiles, 74
    Believers in Jesus Christ, 2n1
    "lawful by nature," 2n1
    Philosophical, 2n1
    Proselyte, 2n1

Subject-Name Index

Wanton pagan, 2n1
Generic article, the, 16, 16n45
Gnostics and Gnosticism, 12,
    13n33, 14, 18, 19, 25, 28,
    29n29, 51, 70, 71
God, 26, 38n11, 44–46, 49, 66, 67,
    69, 70, 75
God's creation design in Genesis,
    17
Good works, 13, 20, 35, 44, 50
Gorday, Peter, 48n21
Gordon, T. David, 4n6
Grace, 43, 44
Graves, Robert, 69n51
Greek mythology, 19, 25, 51
Gregory of Nyssa, 48
Grube, G.M.A., 28n24
Gupta, Nijay, 60, 60nn17–22, 61,
    61nn23–26, 63
Gynecological reproductive
    metaphor, 7, 21, 28

Hades, 29n29
Hagar, 10n23, 23, 24, 25, 76
Hall, Jonathan, 37n7
Hanson, J. Arthur, 69nn49–50
Hapax legomenon, 5
Harrington, D.J., 21n10
Harris, Kamala, 104, 104n18
Haustafeln, 31n37, 98
Hays, Richard, 53n2, 74n66
Hebrew midwives, 6, 22, 25, 39n17
Hebrew Scriptures, 9, 22, 25
Hegesippus, 85
Hellenism, 31
Hellenistic influence, 29, 30,
    31n37, 33, 36n3
Hellenistic setting, 20, 20n9, 73n12
Hellenistic thinking, 25, 28n25,
    31, 36
Hengel, Martin, 31, 31n39
Heracles, 30n33, 111–12
Hermes Trismegisthus, 15n43
Heraclitus, 29n30, 37n9

Hera, 30n33, 40n19
Hermogenes of Tarsus, 68
Heroines of Israel's history, 25
Hesiod, 29n29, 29n31, 37, 38,
    38n14
Hierapolis, 64
Hippocrates of Cos, 111
Hollander, Harm W., 30n33
Holmes, Michael W., 81n3,
    86nn11–14, 89n22
Holy Spirit, 43
Homer, 29n29, 29n30, 37, 38,
    38nn13–14, 40n19
Howard, Virgil, xxii
Hurtado, Larry W., 68n48
Hutchinson, D.S., ix
Huttar, David, 62, 62n31, 63
Hyponoia and *allegoria*, 38n13
Hypostatization, 19, 25, 25n19

Ideas in Plato's thought, 37n10
Image of God, 49
Immortal children, Virtues as,
    26, 31
Institute of Women's Policy
    Research, 93
Intertextual and *intratextual*, 35
Ionia and the Ionian philosophers,
    37–39, 40, 40n19, 51
Ionic dialect of Greek, 38n14
Irenaeus, 88n18
Isaac, 7n15, 23, 25, 47
Isis, 39, 69
Issachar, 7n15

Jacobs, Maretha M., 91n1
Jacob, 22, 24
Jerome, 60
Jerusalem, 75, 76
Jesus movement, 98
Jesus, See Christ
Jew-Gentile dichotomy, 46
Johnson, E. Elizabeth, 53n2
Johnson, Lee A., 80n2

Subject-Name Index

Johnson, Luke Timothy, 14n41, 36n4, 43nn7–8, 44nn10–11, 44n13
John the Baptist, 34, 34n1, 35
Josephus, 38n14
Judah, 7n15
Judaism, 13n33, 31, 33, 102
Julia, 58, 64
Junia and Andronicus, 57, 58, 60–64
Junias, 59

Keener, Craig S., 65n40
Kelly, J.N.D., 45n16
Kennedy, George, 39n15, 68n47
Kinetic concept of virtue, 28
Koinè dialect of Greek, 38n14

Laconian boy, 102
Ladner, Joyce A., 93
Laird, Benjamin, 80n2, 88n16
Landerholm, Savanah N., xxii
Laodicea, 55, 64, 74
Larger literary context, 8
Lawgiver, the, 22n14
Layton, Bentley, 18n1
Leah, 24, 25
Liefield, Walter, 12n29
Linus, co-worker of Paul, 80
Linus, bishop of Rome, 85
Lin, Yii-Jan, 61, 61n27, 62, 62n28, 62n30, 62nn32–33, 63, 63nn34–39
Literal "plain sense" reading, 47
Literary world of Paul, 2, 106, 113
Littré, Emilie, 111
Livingstone, E.A., 5n9
Lodge, John G., 53n2
Lois and Eunice, 54
Lombard, Peter, 60
Long, A.A., 37n7
Luke-Acts, author of, 39
Luke, 80
Lund, H.G., 38n12

Luther, Martin, 48, 48n22, 49n23
LXX, 58, 59

Macedonia, 83
Male-female dichotomy, 46, 72, 74, 77
Manoah, 21n10
Marcion of Sinope, 89
Marcus, Ralph, 26n21
Mark, 80
Marshall, I. Howard, 10n19, 12n29, 45n15, 46nn19–20
Martin, Clarice J., 31n37, 95, 95n6, 97nn7–8, 98n10, 99n11, 100n14, 101n14
Mary Magdalene, 64
Mary of Nazareth, 13, 70
Mary of Rome, 64
McDonald, L.M., 39n16
Median annual income for Black women, 94
Meeks, Wayne, 52n28
Men, Ephesian, 9, 11
Menander, 29n32
Messiah, 17
Method of interpretation, Philo's, 6n12
Metaphor, 3,4, 7 n15, 9, 38n14, 40, 41n20, 47, 78
Metaphorical interpretation, 6n12, 10, 10n22, 15, 22n14, 41, 48, 78
Metaphorical reference, 9, 21
Metzger, Bruce, 58, 58n9
Midwifery, 40
Michael the archangel, 33
Miller, Jeff, 106n3
Mind and Pleasure, 2n1, 24
Mitchell, Matthew W., 30n33
Mosaic law, 2n1
Mother of Paul, 75, 76
Mounce, William D., 10n21
Mouton, Elna, 107, 107nn5–6, 108nn7–11, 109n13

127

Subject-Name Index

Muratorian Canon, 89, 89n21
Murphy-O'Connor, Jerome, 66n41

Natalistic concept of virtue, 27, 28, 38, 39
Natalistic language, 29n30, 29n32, 37, 38n11, 41n20, 51
Nereus, the old man of the sea, 38
Nereus, the sister of, 64
Nero, 80
Nicomachean Ethics, 28
Night (as a Greek god), 20n8
Nine Muses, The, 20n5
Noah, 7–8, 21 n.10, 22, 28n25
Nympha, 55, 74

Oceanus, 29n30, 37
O' Day, Gail, xxii
Odell-Scott, David W., 66, 66nn41–42, 67n43, 68n45
Odyssey, The, 29n29
Offspring of the soul, 7n15, 8n16
One sentence dismissal, the, 106, 107, 110
Onesimus, 21n12, 56, 100
Onesiphoros, 55, 80
Origen of Alexandria, 4n9, 60, 61
Orr, William F. 30n33

Padgett, Alan, 3, 4, 5, 9, 11, 11n26, 12, 13, 13n33–34, 15
Papyrus 46, 58
Parry, Robin, xxii
Particular article, the, 16, 16n46
Passion of Perpetua and Felicity, 60
Pastoral Epistles, 4, 11n24, 21, 44, 46, 47, 54, 55, 79, 80–84, 88–90, 96
"Patriarchal imagery and language," 72
Patriarchy, 73, 78
Patron, 56, 71
Patterson, Orlando, 100n13

Paul the Apostle, 1, 2, 17, 21, 22, 29n33, 30n33, 53–60, 63–65, 71, 72, 75–83, 96, 99, 101, 102, 105, 106
Pauline corpus, 10, 53, 55, 64, 87n15, 88n16
Pausanias, 41n20
Pedens, 80
Pederasty, condemnation of, 27n22
Pelagius, 48
Perriman, Andrew C., 3, 4,5, 11, 11n26, 12, 12n29, 13, 13n35, 15
Persecution of the church, 85, 86
Persis, 64
Peters, F.E., 37n8, 38n13
Peter the Apostle, 86, 89, 99
Philemon, 100
Philo of Alexandria, 1, 2, 4n9, 6, 8, 15n43, 22–26, 27nn22–23, 28, 30, 31, 37,38, 38n14, 47, 48, 50, 51, 101, 102
Phoebe, 55, 56
Phoebus, see Apollo
Plain sense reading, 47
Plato, 27, 28, 29n30, 30, 37, 38, 38nn13–14, 39, 40, 40n19, 47, 48, 50,51
Plato, *Republic* 588A-589B as NHL text, 28n29
Platonic influence, 28, 28n29, 50, 51
Polycarp of Smyrna, 84, 87, 87n15, 88, 88n18–19, 89
Polyxena, 102
Porter, Stanley E., 11n26, 13, 13nn36–37
Postnatal or post-generative relationship, 15, 21
Prefigurative relationship, 3, 4
Pre-Pauline baptismal formula, 71, 73, 74, 77
Prior, M., 35n3

SUBJECT-NAME INDEX

Prisca and Aquila, 55, 56, 64, 77, 80
Priscilla, see Prisca and Aquila
Pronouns, equivalence between, 9
Prosōpopoeia and *ēthopoeia*, 68, 78
Proto-Gnostic, 12, 25
Prototypical relationship, 9
Pythagoras, 37n9

Quinn, Jerome D., 35n3
Quintilian, 68
Qumran, 32

Rackham, H, 28n28
Räisänen, Heikki, 53
Ramelli, Ilaria L.E., 79n1
Rachel, 22, 25
Racial and gender discrimination, 94
Rebekah, 15n43, 24, 25
Reeves, Rodney, 82, 83, 83nn4-9
Reformation, 48
Religio-philosophical context, 8, 51
Repentance, the daughter of God, 33
Resurrection of Jesus Christ, 57
Richards, E. Randolph, 82, 83, 83nn4-9
Robinson, William C., Jr.,19n4
Roman Empire, 98, 99, 102
Rome, 55, 61, 83, 84, 89, 100
Rouse, W.H.D., 28n24
Rubinkiewicz, R., 38n12
Ruether, Rosemary Radford, 73, 73nn61-64, 78
Rufus, the mother of, 64

Salvation, 5n11, 6, 15, 45-48, 75
  Eschatological, 42, 43, 43n5, 44, 45, 96
  Realized, 43, 43n5, 44, 45, 96
Samson, 21n10
Sanders, E.P., 53n1

San Diego Natural History Museum, 32n41
Sarah, 10n23, 23, 24, 25, 26n21, 47, 76
Saved through childbearing, 3, 46, 48, 49, 52, 91, 95, 96
Saving faith,54
Schaff, Philip, 50n25
Schneemelcher, Wilhelm, 70n53
Schofield, Malcolm, 37n7, 38, 38nn11-12
Scholer, David, xxii, 10n22
Schreiner, Thomas R., 15n41
Schüssler Fiorenza, Elisabeth, 71, 71nn55-56, 72, 72nn57-60, 73, 77, 77n67, 78
Scopello, Maddalena, 19n4
Scripture as instrument of liberation or oppression, 96
Scripture interpretation, 97, 101, 103
Shepherd of Hermas, 81
Similar pattern of thinking, 6
Simon and Cleobius, 70
Skalko, John J., 55n4
Slavery, 2n1, 65, 71, 76, 97, 98, 99, 100-102
Slaves, 2n1, 72-74, 98
Slave masters, 2n1, 73, 98
Slave traders (*andrapodistais*), 99
Smyth, Herbert Weir, 16nn45-46, 38n14
Social hierarchy, 65
Socrates, 26, 27, 29n30, 37n6, 40, 41, 41n20
Solevag, Anna Rebecca, 106nn3-4
Solon the Athenian statesman, 26, 27
Sophocles, 38n14, 102
Soteriological description, 42
Soul as female, the, 27, 27n23, 28n24
Sound doctrine, 43, 44
Sōphrosynē, 5, 6n11

129

Southern Methodist University, xxii
Spartacus, 100
Spirit and flesh, 2n1
Standhartinger, Angela, 52n28
Staples, Robert, 93n3
Stobaeus, Joannes, 111
Streete, Gail P.C., 105nn1–2
Strife (as a Greek goddess), 20, 20n8
Stuckenbruck, Loren T., 71n54
Sumney, Jerry, ix
Synecdoche, childbearing as, 13
Syncretism, 14n41
Syntyche, See Euodia and Syntyche.

Tartarus, 29n29
Tat, see Hermes Trismegisthus
Teknogonia, 5, 14, 16, 20, 31, 54, 111–13
Tethys, 29n30, 37
Text of terror, 91
Thackeray, H. St. J., 59
Thales, 37n9
Theaetetus, 29n30, 40, 41
Themis, 20, 20n5
Theodore of Mopsuestia, 48
Theodoret, 60
Therapeutae, Therapeutrides, 25, 31, 31n40, 32
Third Servile War, 100
Thompson, Lisa L, 93, 93n4
Three Fates, The, 20n5
Thurston, Bonnie Bowman, 45n17
Tilford, Nicole L., ix
Timothy, co-worker of Paul, 31, 53, 54, 56, 80, 81, 82, 83
Titus, co-worker of Paul, 56, 80, 81, 82, 83, 88
Titus, emperor of Rome, 85
Tolbert, Mary Ann 103n16

Towner, Philip H., 10n19, 12n29, 43n4, 45n15, 46nn19–20, 87n15, 88n17
Truth as mother, 37n10
Trophimus, 80
Tryphena and Tryphosa, 64
Tychicus, 55, 56, 80
Typology, typological interpretation, 3,4, 4n8, 9, 10n23

Universal law of creation, 9
Urbanus, 56

van der Hout, Gijsbert, 30n33
van Wolde, Ellen, 107, 107nn5–6, 108nn7–11, 109n13
Vermes, Geza, 32n43
Vespasian, 85
Virtue, Virtues, 2, 23, 25, 28n26, 35, 44
Virtue and vice lists, 30–31
Virtues-bearing, 51, 54
Virtue ethics, Hellenistic 6, 30, 45, 47, 51
Virtues as children, 2, 3, 7,8, 15, 18–22, 25, 28, 31–36, 41, 96, 105, 106
Vices as children, 2, 7, 18–20, 25, 31–33, 36

Wacker, W.C., 35n3
Wallace, Daniel, 61, 61n26
Walther, James Arthur, 30n33
Waterfield, Robin, 37n7
Waters, Deborah Tarver, v, xxii
Waters, Kenneth L. Sr., 57n6, 66n42, 68n44, 108
Watson, Wilfred G.E., 32nn42–44
Weems, Renita J., 92n2
Welch, P.G., 39n18
Wessels, Johannes M., 106n3
West, Gerald, 91n1
Whitaker, G.H., 6n13, 24n16

Subject-Name Index

Wimer, Matthew, xxii
Wilson, R. McL., 70n53
Wisdom as mother, 15n43, 34, 34n1, 35, 35n2
Wisse, Frederik, 19n3
Wolters, Al, 58, 58n7, 58n10, 59, 59nn11–15, 60, 60n16, 61, 63
Womb of the soul, 27n23
Women, 2, 10, 10n22, 13, 26
    African American, 92–97, 101, 103, 104
    Dardanian, 102
    Ephesian, 3, 6, 9, 11, 13, 16, 21, 22
    In the Christian mission, 55, 64, 65, 71, 72
    Married and unmarried, 72, 77, 78
    Ministry and leadership of, 66, 71, 72, 74, 78, 107–8
    Native American, 93
    Subordination of, 75–77
Wright, N.T., 74n65

Xanthians, 102
Xenophanes, 37, 37n9, 38

Yonge, C.D., ix, 6n13, 24n16, 26n20
Young, Frances Margaret, 20n9, 42nn1–2, 43nn6, 43n9, 44n14

Zehr, Paul M., 106n3
Zenas, 80
Zeus, 20, 20n5, 29n29, 30n33
Zoe (as a Gnostic archon), 18

Ancient Document Index

OLD TESTAMENT/ HEBREW BIBLE

Genesis

1:27	49
2:7–25	11
2:10–14	5n11
2—3	107, 108, 109
3	104
3:1–21	4, 9
3:1–7	3
3:15	13
3:16	3, 5, 15n42, 24, 26
6:1–4	70
6:9	8
11:29	22n14
30:2	7n15

Exodus

1:21	6, 39n17
14:10—32:35	10n23

Deuteronomy

5:3	7n15
7:13	7n15
24:16	10
25:4	2n1
28:4	7n15
28:11	7n15
28:18	7n15
30:9	7n15

1 Chronicles

7:14	22n14

Job

38:29	38n11
42:6	33

Psalms

7:14	33

Proverbs

8:19	35
8:32–36	15n43, 35n2

Isaiah

13:18	7n15
54:1	76

Jeremiah

31:29–30	10

Ezekiel

14:6	33
18:1–4	10
18:30	33

Hosea

9:16	7n15

PSEUDEPIGRAPHA AND APOCRYPHA

2 Baruch

62.5	7n15
73.7	7n15

3 Baruch

8.5 (Slavonic and Greek)	30
13.4 (Greek)	30

1 Enoch

6.1–8	70
7.1–6	70
8.1–4	70

2 Enoch

71.11	7n15

Apocalypse of Abraham

14.6	38n12

Corpus Hermeticum

13.3	15n43

Joseph and Aseneth

15.7–8	33

Jubilees

20.9	7n15
28.16	7n15

Letter of Aristeas

260	35

Liber Antiquitatum Biblicarum

42.1–3	21n10
50.2	7n15
55.4	7n15

Odes of Solomon

11.1–3	6n14
11.16a–21	21n10

Psalms of Solomon

14.2–5	21n10

Wisdom of Solomon

7:22–23	30
8:7	30, 35
14:25–26	30

Testament of Abraham

6.5	7n15
8.6	7n15

Testament of Judah

16.1	30

Testament of Levi

17.11	30

NEW TESTAMENT

Matthew

1:8–11	59
3:8	33
7:16–20	21n11

Ancient Document Index

9:13	33
10:16	57
11:19	35
12:33	21n11
15:19	30
28:9–10	64

Luke

1:42	7n15
3:38	17, 17n51
7:35	34, 35, 41n20
8:3	56
10:1	61
10:3	57

John

3:3–7	41n20
13:20	57
17:18	57
20:17–18	64
20:21	57
21:20–24	57

Acts

1:21–22	57
1:22	57
16:1	54n3
17:28a	29n32
17:28b	29n32, 41n19
18:1–4	55
18:2	55
18:18–22	55
18:18	55
18:24–26	55
18:26	55
19:24–41	39

Romans

1:3	76
1:16	46, 52
1:18–32	2n1
1:26–27	27n22
1:29–31	30n34
2:6–8	45
2:10	46
2:25–29	2n1
2:12–16	2n1
3:28	52
3:30	46
4:9–12	2n1
5:3–5	30n34
5:10	17
5:14	17
5:18	17
6:14–23	102
6:21–22	6
6:22	52
7:4–5	6
7:7–12	52
8:1–17	2n1
8:24	52
9:5	45
9:26–27	75
10:9–10	52
11:17–24	10
11:13	2n1
11:25	2n1
12:9–21	44
12:13	44
13:10	52
13:11–14	44
13:13	30n34
15:13	44
15:19	76
15:25	76
15:26	76
15:31	76
16:1–2	55
16:1	80
16:3	55, 56, 78
16:5	55
16:6	64
16:7	57–62
16:9	56
16:12	64
16:13	64
16:15	58, 64

Romans (continued)

16:21	56
16:22	80

1 Corinthians

1:11	55, 74
1:17	57
2:14	44
3:5	55
3:9	56
4:15	76
6:9	27n22, 30n34
7:17–24	2n1
7:17–20	74
7:21–24	74, 98, 99
7:23	99
7:26–31	78
7:28	77
7:29–31	99
7:32–35	77
8:1–3	67
8:1	70
9:1	57
9:5	78
9:9	2n1
10:1–13	11n23
10:1–11	10
10:1–5	2n1
10:4	11n23
10:6	10n23
10:11	10n23
10:23	68
11:1–16	71
11:2–16	71n54
11:3–16	68, 69, 74
11:3–10	65, 67
11:3–9	66n41
11:5–7	49, 50
11:10	69, 70, 71
11:11–12	66n41, 67
11:13–15	65, 66n41, 67
11:16	66n41, 67
12:13	72–74, 77, 100
12:28–29	57
13:1	69
13:4–7	10, 30n34, 44
13:13	44
14:33b–36	72
14:34–36	66n41, 68
14:34–35	66n41, 67
14:34–36	71
14:34	65, 69
14:36	66n41, 67, 67n43
15:3–11	63, 76
15:5–11	57
15:6	57
15:8	29n33, 41n20
15:21–22	17
15:22	17
15:24–27	99
15:33	29n32
15:45	17
15:58	44
16:3	76
16:8–11	36
16:10	56
16:14	44
16:19	55
16:21	80

2 Corinthians

3:6	55
3:7	75
3:13	75
5:10	45
6:4–5	56
6:6–7	30n34
7:6	56
7:13	56
8:23	56, 57
10:9–10	80
10:12	63
11:23–33	56

Galatians

1:11—2:10	63
1:13—2:10	63
1:15–16	75

Ancient Document Index

1:16	57	6:9	98
1:17	76	6:12–17	10
1:18	76	6:31	56
2:1	76		
2:16	52	**Philippians**	
3:7	75	1:1	55
3:26	75	1:11	6–7
3:27–28	65	1:13	80
3:28	46, 65, 71–75, 77, 100, 102	2:12	52
		2:25	57, 80
3:29	75	2:25–30	56
4:4	76	2:30	57
4:1–11	102	4:2	56, 64
4:19	21, 41n20, 76	4:3	56, 64, 86
4:21–31	76, 102	4:8–9	30n34
4:22–27	10, 10n23	4:22	80
4:24	2 n1, 10n23		
4:25–26	76	**Colossians**	
4:26–27	41n20	1:6	7
4:27	76	1:7	55, 56
5:1–15	102	1:10	7
5:1–12	2n1	1:23	55
5:1	100	1:25	55
5:6	75	3:6	75
5:16–25	2n1	3:8–9	30n34
5:19–31	30n34	3:11	74, 77, 100
5:22–26	21n11	3:12–17	30n34
5:22–25	6, 44	3:18—4:1	31n37
5:22–23	30n34	3:22—4:1	98
6:8	44	4:1	98
6:10	44	4:7	55, 56, 80
6:11	80	4:8	56
		4:9	80
Ephesians		4:10	58
2:2	75	4:13	64
2:5	52	4:15	55, 74
2:8	52	4:16	80
4:11	57	4:18	80
4:21–24	44		
4:25–32	44	**1 Thessalonians**	
5:6	75	3:2	56
5:8–11	6	5:3	41n20
5:22—6:4	31n37	5:5	75
6:5–9	98	5:27	80

2 Thessalonians

1:4	44
1:5	44
2:2–3	80
2:13–17	44
3:17	80

1 Timothy

1:1	16n44, 45, 80
1:2–3	82
1:2	43, 44
1:3	36, 80, 83
1:4	44
1:5	16n44, 22
1:8–11	52
1:9–11	99
1:10	27n22
1:11	16n44
1:12–17	76, 81
1:13–14	43
1:14	16n44, 44
1:16	54
1:18	82
1:19	22
1:3–7,	9
1:3–6	12
1:5–6	6, 8
1:5	45
1:9–10	30n34
1:16	44, 45
1:17	85
1:19	6, 8, 44
1:20	9, 12
2:1	46
2:2	45
2:3	16n44, 45
2:3–6	45
2:4	42, 43, 46, 46n19
2:6	43, 46
2:7	46, 85
2:8—3:11	10
2:8–12	46
2:8–10	9
2:8–15	107
2:8	84
2:9–10	84, 85
2:9	10n22, 11
2:10	8, 10n22, 13, 35
2:11–15	1, 2n1, 3, 7–9, 10n22, 11–13, 25, 39, 51, 54, 65, 66n41, 78, 79, 91, 92, 95–97, 103, 104, 106, 108, 109, 109n13
2:11	10n22
2:12	12, 39
2:13–15	17, 85, 107
2:14–15	17
2:12	12
2:13	10n22
2:14	10n22, 15n42
2:15	2, 3, 5, 6, 9, 10n22, 13, 14, 14n40, 15n42, 16, 16n44, 17, 19, 20–22, 26, 30, 30n34, 31, 34, 35, 40, 41n20, 42, 44, 45, 47, 48–51, 54, 78, 96, 106, 113
3:2–7	30n34
3:2–4	44, 45
3:2	46
3:4–5	31n37
3:5	87
3:8–13	44, 87
3:8–10	30n34
3:8	55
3:9	16n44, 44
3:11–12	30n34, 46
3:11	55n5
3:12	31n37, 55
3:16	16n44, 46
3:14–15	9
4:1	16n44
4:3	13

4:6	16n44, 44	1:10	43, 45
4:8–10	44	1:11	46
4:8	16n44	1:12	44
4:10	46, 54	1:13	44
4:12	8, 16n44, 44, 52, 81	1:14	43
		1:15–18	81
4:14	45	1:16–17	83
4:15–16	45	1:18	36, 80
4:16	9, 43, 54	2:2	43, 44
5:5	50	2:3–6	11n24
5:9–10	13, 45	2:5	44, 81
5:10	5n10	2:8	76
5:11–15	12	2:10	16n44, 43
5:14	5n10	2:10–13	42
5:15	10n22	2:11	44
5:18	2n1, 9	2:12	87
5:23	82	2:14–18	12
5:25	44, 45	2:15	16n44
6:1–2	2n1, 31n37, 97, 98, 109n13	2:19	9, 44, 46
		2:20–21	11
6:2	98	2:21	43, 44
6:7	87	2:22	6, 8, 22, 30n34, 44, 45
6:10	87		
6:11–12	44	2:25	43
6:11	30n34, 44, 45	3:2–5	30n34
6:12	16, 43, 43n5, 54	3:6–9	12
6:13	43	3:8	9
6:14–15	42	3:10–17	81
6:18–19	44, 45	3:10–11	81
6:18	43, 44	3:10	45
6:19	42	3:15–16	43
6:20	12, 19, 70	3:15	16n44, 43, 44, 52, 54
2 Timothy		3:16	9
1:1	80	3:17	44
1:2	44, 82	4:1	42, 43
1:9	52	4:3	16n44
1:5–7	44	4:5	45
1:5–6	45	4:6–17	81
1:5	44, 54, 54n3	4:6–8	11n24
1:7	43	4:6	80
1:8–10	45	4:7–8	45
1:9–10	44	4:7	44
1:9	43	4:8	16n44, 42, 43

139

2 Timothy (continued)

4:10	87
4:12	36
4:14	12
4:15–18	56
4:16–17	83
4:17	43, 46
4:18	42, 43
4:19	55
4:21	64
4:22	43

Titus

1:1	80
1:2	42
1:3	45
1:4–5	82
1:4	44, 45
1:5–9	55n5
1:5	80, 83
1:7–9	30n34, 45
1:12	29n32
1:13	43, 44
2:2	30n34, 44
2:3–8	45
2:3–5	30n34
2:3–4	45
2:6–8	30n34
2:9–10	30n34, 31n37, 98
2:9	98
2:10	45
2:11–12	8, 30n34, 52
2:11–14	44, 45
2:11	43, 43n5, 46
2:13	42, 45
2:14	43
3:1–2	30n34
3:1	80, 84
3:3–7	44
3:3	30n34
3:4–8	45
3:4	45
3:5	16n44, 43
3:6	45
3:7	42, 43n5, 52
3:8	44
3:9	12
3:12	56, 81
3:14	7
3:15	43

Philemon

2	55, 74
8–21	98
10	21n12, 41n20
12	56, 80
16	100
19	80
23	58

Hebrews

12:14	52

James

1:15	36, 41n20
1:18	41n20
3:17	35

1 Peter

1:3	41n20
2:12	99
2:18	98

2 Peter

1:16–19	57
2:4	70
3:15–16	80

1 John

1:1–4	57
4:2–3	70

2 John

7	70

Jude

6	70
14	17, 17n51

Revelation

12:1–6	41n20
18:1–13	100

DEAD SEA SCROLLS

Hodayot or Thanksgiving Hymns from Qumran Cave 1

1QH10.7–9	32n42
1QH13.30	32n42
1QH17.35	32n44
1QH20.8	32n42

War Scrolls from Qumran Cave 1

1QM 1.11	32n44
1QM 3.6	32n44
1QM17.8	32n44

Rule of the Community from Qumran Cave 4

4QSe 3.10	32n44

Texts from Qumran Cave 4

4Q168.1	32n42
4Q424. Fr.3	32
4Q427.2.7–8	32n42
4Q429.4	32n42
4Q502.1–3.8	32n44
4Q502.1–3.6	32n44
4Q511.10.4	32n44

GRECO-ROMAN WRITINGS

Appian

Bella civilia

2.14	56

Historia romana

1.539–60	100

Apuleius

Metamorphoses

10.35	69
11.2	39
11.10	69

Aristotle

De virtutibus et vitiis

2.1–7	30
3.1–8	30
4.1—5.7	30
6.1—7.14	30
8.1–4	30

Ethica eudemia

2.3.4	30, 30n35

Ethica nichomaches

2.2.7–9	30
3.6.1—5.3.17	30
4.3.33–34	28
5.2.13	30
6.13.1–8	28n27
7.5.3	27n22
7.7.7	27n22

Ancient Document Index

Historia Animalium IX (VII)

582a.25	112

Metaphysica

1,3.19—1.5.28	37n9
1.3.29–36	37
8.1.1—8.3.30	37n9

Politicia

1:12	31n37, 98

Callimachus

Hymnus in Apollinem

60	40n19

Hymnus in Diana

20–22	39

Cassius Dio

Historia Roma

74	56

Cicero

In Pisonem

25	56

Diodorus Siculus

Bibliotheca historica

4.9.4	30n33

Cleanthes

Hymn to Zeus

4	29n32

Galen

Corpus Medicorum Graecorum

5.9.1	111n1
112.48.10	113

Hermogenes of Tarsus

Progymnasmata

9	68

Hesiod

Theogony

76–79	20n5
116	29n31
218–19	20n5
224–32	20, 31n38
233–39	38
909	20
922	40n19
945	20

Hipprocrates of Cos

Letters

17.84	111

Homer

Iliad

6.147	29n31
6.484	29n31
11.270–71	40n19
14.201–2	29n30
14.246	29n30
16.184	40n19
16.187	40n19
19.103	40n19
19.118	30n33

Ancient Document Index

19.119	30n33, 40n19	2.45–52	23n15
		2.60	24

Odyssey

4.363	29n31
4.392	29n31
6.107	29n31
9.355	29n31
12.183–94	29n31
14.258	29n31

Pausanias

Graeciae description

2.35.11	41n20

Philo

De Abrahamo

52	28n26
54	20n6
99	22n14, 23
131	2n1, 22n14
147	22n14

De aeternitate mundi

17	29n31
18	29n31
37	29n31
132	29n31

De agricultura

9–11	7n15
23	7n15
25	7n15
97	22n14
157	22n14

De cherubim

1.21	22n14
1.25	22n14

De confusion linguarum

21	30, 30n36
49	15n43

De congressu eruditionis gratia

4	23
6	7n15, 23, 35
13–23	23,
40	21n10
43–44	22n14
49	35n2
98	23
129	24, 26n21, 35
180	22n14

De ebrietate

8	21n10
23	5n11, 30
165	25n18

De fuga et inventione

50–52	15n43, 35
181	22n14

De gigantibus

4	7n15, 21n10
5	7, 8, 8n17, 47

De Iosepho

1	28n26

De migratione Abrahami

34	27n23
125	7n15
139–40	7n15
140	26n21
156	29n31

De migratione Abrahami (continued)

195	29n31
203	22n14
205–6	7n15
205	21n10
214	39n17

De mutatione nominum

73	7n15
77–79	23
98–100	21n10
132–33	24
161	7n15
189	8
224	7n15

De opificio mundi

154–55	7n15, 22n14
164	6n12

De plantatione

36	22n14
77	7n15
106	7n15
126	7n15
132	7n15, 21n10
134–38	7n15
134–37	24
136	7n15, 21n10

De posteritate Caini

10	7n15
52	30
100	22n14
128	5n11, 30

De sacrificiis Abelis et Caini

4	24
32	30
103–4	7n15

De sobrietate

28	21n10
65	7n15

De somnis

1.37	7n15
1.167–68	28n26
2.75–77	7n15
2.139	27n23
2.174	20n6
2.207	2n1, 22n14
2.266	30
2.260	22n14
2.272	7n15

De specialibus legibus

1.1–11	2n1
1.36–37	2n1
1.51–54	2n1
1.327	2n1, 22n14
2.29	7n15, 22n14
3.39	27n22

De virtutibus

14–16	5n11, 47
145	2n1

De vita contemplative

2	25
40–41	29n31
57–61	27n22
68	7n15, 26

Legatio ad Gaium

80	29n31

Legum allegoriae

1.45	7n15
1.49	7n15
1.63–72	5n11
1.75	24

Ancient Document Index

2.22–41	2n1
2.82	23, 23n15, 35
3.3	6, 22, 39n17
3.68	23
3.88–89	24
3.180–81	22
3.198–221	3
3.198	24
3.217	25
3.221	25
3.216	24
3.217	35
3.220	24
3.246–47	25

Quaestiones et solutiones in Genesin

1.37	24
1.49	7n15, 25n17
1.52	6n12, 22n14
2.36	22n14
2.37	22n14
3.3	29n31
3.10	7n15, 26n21
3.16	29n31
3:24	22n14
3.25	22n14
3.32	22n14
3.54	7n15

Quid rerum divinarum heres sit

50	22n14, 24

Quod deterius potiori insidari solent

127	26n21
167	22n14

Quod Deus sit immutabilis

4	7n15
79	30
95	22n14

117–18	8, 8n17, 28n25, 47
166	7 n15
180	7n15

Quod omnis probus liber sit

8–10	102
10–18	2n1
10	101
16–18	102
19	102
20–21	102
36–41	2n1
36	102
41	102
70	7n15, 30
82	22n14
114	102
115	102
116	102
118–20	102
137	102
160	7n15

Philostratus

Heroikos

7.8	35, 37n10

Plato

Cratylus

396B-C	29n30
397E–398A	29n30
402B-C	29n30, 37

Laches

198B	30

Leges

2.658D	29n30

Ancient Document Index

Lysis
215C   29n30

Menexenus
238A   29n30

Minos
318E–319D   29n30

Phaedrus
105D   28
106B   28
107C   28

Protagoras
349B   30

Respublica
3.389D   5n11, 47
4.427E   30
6.18E   35, 37n9
6.496A   22n13
4.419A–445E   5n11
10.609B   30

Symposium
203B–C   37n10
206C   26
206D   40n19, 41n20
209A–D   27
209C   27n22
209D–E   27, 47

Theaetetus
149B–151E   40
150D   40
150E   40
151A–C   41
152D–E   37
152E   29n30

Theages
129D   37n6

Timaeus
40E–41A   29n30, 37

Plutarch

Crassus
8–11   100

Pseudo-Dionysius

Ecclesiastical Hierarchy
6.1–3   31n40

Pseudo-Phocylides
194   25n19

Quintilian

Institutio Oratoria
6.1.25   68

Stobaeus, Joannes

Eclogues
11.94–7   112

EARLY CHRISTIAN WRITINGS

3 Corinthians
1:2–15   70

Ancient Document Index

Augustine

De Civitate Dei

4.20–24	25n19
8.2	37n9
10:3	50
18.37	37n9
19.4.4	6n11

De Trinitate

12.7.11	48

Clement of Alexandria

Stromata

3.12.90	48

Clement of Rome

1 Clement

1:1	86
2:7	84
5:4–7	89
5:5–7	89n21
5:2	86
6:1–2	86
7:1	86
29:1	84
33:4–6	85
33:7	84, 85
60:4	85
61:2	85

Eusebius

Historia ecclesiastica

2.22.7–8	89n21
3.13–15	85n10
3.21.1	85n10

Irenaeus

Adversus haereses

III.3.3	85n10
III.3.4	88n18

Muratorian Canon

38–39	89n21

Polycarp of Smyrna

Letter to the Philippians

3:2	88
4:1	87
5:2	87
7:2	88
9:2	87
11:2	87
12:1	88

GNOSTIC LITERATURE

Apocalypse of Adam

6:1	21n10

Asclepius

21–29	29n29
75	29n29

Concept of our Great Power

37	29n29
41	29n29
42	29n29
43–44	28n29

Ancient Document Index

Exegesis of the Soul

127	28n29
134	28n29
134:30	19
136	29n29
137	29n29

Interpretation of Knowledge

13	29n29

On the Origin of the World

106–7	18, 31n38

Paraphrase of Shem

23:30	19

Plato, Republic 588A–589B

49	29n29

Teachings of Silvanus, The

99	28n29

Tripartite Tractate, The

75–77	28n29
104–5	70

Valentinian Exposition, A

37	28n29
39	28n29

www.ingramcontent.com/pod-product-compliance
Lightning Source LLC
Chambersburg PA
CBHW050819160426
43192CB00010B/1826